the ART of NOTHING

Decision Making on an Artist's Quest

By Jim Brock

Published by Jim Brock

Grand Junction, Colorado

First Edition

Library of Congress Control Number: 2014907080

ISBN-13: 978-0-9816318-2-0

ISBN-10: 0-9816318-2-7

Published by

Jim Brock

P. O. Box 141

Grand Junction, CO 81502

For Judy, Jenny, and Jackie

Preface

This story is a continuation of an artist's journey found in
The Color of Nothing and *The Other Side of Nothing.*

What should an artist paint? What he wants to paint,
or what is consistent?

The Art of Nothing

Nowat is an old hippie artist who begins his paintings by sloshing watercolor around on a large piece of paper with a great Chinese brush made of feathers.

Yes, feathers.

And he's usually high at the time.

Wasted.

Schnockered.

When he's seemingly satisfied with the sloshing, he stumbles into bed.

The next morning, after he's sobered up, he sits in front of the paper and stares at it. Sporadically, he stands up, picks up a box of children's watercolors and a small brush, and points them at the paper, often for several minutes. Then he grabs a wad of paper towels and throws them at the paper. He even kicks the jug of water sitting by his chair. Finally, he yells something completely unintelligible, sits down, and resumes staring.

This can go on for hours.

I know.

I've watched him.

Sitting.

Staring.

Pointing.

Grabbing.

Throwing.

Kicking.

Yelling.

Sitting.

Staring.

Pointing.

Grabbing.

Throwing.

Kicking.

Yelling.

After I got to know him, I asked why he was so active. I understood the meditative part, but why all the action?

He replied that he points, grabs, throws, kicks, and yells to get everybody's attention. After all, the paints, brush, towels, and water need to see what they have to do. He says they are quite shy. They rarely do things on their own. So they need to be reminded of the important part each plays.

Whatever works?

I guess.

Ultimately, he rises; collects the brush, the paper towels that have been strewn about the room, the box of children's watercolors, and a jug of water; and finishes the painting very quickly—usually within just a few minutes.

Then he formally bows and thanks everything—the brush, the paper towels, the box of watercolors, the jug of water, and finally, the painting.

And the painting is marvelous.

***

Nowat—pronounced "nowwhat," as one word—was given that name by an old spiritual guru for reasons that Nowat can't seem to remember. As I said, Nowat is an old hippie—shorts, sandals, scruffy beard, and dirty blond ponytail—straight out of the nineteen sixties. At one time, he may have been quite handsome, but life and a little too much weed have taken their toll. Now he wears a silly grin, and has an infectious chuckle and bright blue eyes that belie his age and condition.

Our first meeting was really not by chance. Call it destiny, fate, luck, providence, or magic—whatever it was, I had to meet him.

I was sitting in my favorite neighborhood coffee shop, adjusting to morning, when he entered and came directly to my table. I had never met him—didn't know him until that moment.

He stood silently for a few seconds, just grinning and staring at me.

Then he spoke.

"Yo, Dude," he said.

"Ah…yo, yourself," I replied.

"Let us, ah, like *go*," he said, pointing to the door of the shop.

Then he turned around and walked toward it.

"Hey, wait a minute!" I yelled.

But the coffee shop door was now blue. It had been mousy brown—a basic wood door—but now…

I knew that door.

I had seen it before.

I had to go.

Didn't I?

***

Those of you who know my history are aware that blue doors have been important to me. Whenever I have needed something—or someone—a blue door has appeared in my path. I can choose to ignore it or open it and go through—my choice. But what I have always needed has been behind that door.

So you would think that I would always choose to go *through* the door.

Yeah.

Sure I do.

I always jump into the unknown with a great deal of enthusiasm.

Yeah.

Courage versus prudence.

Prudence is easier.

But experience has shown me that I shouldn't ignore a blue door. There are consequences.

So, off I go…again.

Stupid?

Possibly.

Probably says my head.

But maybe not.

At one time, I thought these azure happenings to be enchanted—in some way not reality. But their impact on my life has been significant…actually more than significant: *spectacular*.

So maybe the blue door events are mystical *and* real.

Maybe reality constantly offers me what I need, albeit in odd ways.

All I need to do is choose to accept it.

Maybe.

Why don't I just get it—what I need?

Why do I have to choose?

Why not a window instead of a door?

Why is it blue and not red?

Confusion still reigns.

Whatever.

***

I ran after Nowat toward the door.

On the way, I looked around. Nobody else seemed to notice that the door had changed. At least nobody was looking at it strangely.

Hmm…?

Anyway, I ran through the door trying to catch up with Nowat…and ran into nothing.

Nothing.

There was nothing there.

I really mean nothing.

Just white.

No shades, no shadows.

Just white.

Everywhere.

No walls.

No ceiling.

I guess there was a floor because I was standing on something. But I couldn't see it.

Even the door I had come through was gone.

One of my good friends always says "too much white" when she sees one of my paintings for the first time. But this was actually "too much white."

Scared?

Yeah!

I don't normally admit to being afraid, but this was not one of those times. I was terrified. I could admit it.

Then I noticed Nowat. He was standing at what I guessed was about 10 feet in front of me. He was looking at me with a great smile on his face and his hands up in the air.

"Awesome! Awesome! Awesome!"

He kept repeating over and over, "Awesome! Awesome!"

Somehow, his talking and smile helped to reduce my fear…somewhat.

After recovering a little from the circumstance, I shouted, "Hey! Hey!"

But he kept talking.

"Awesome! Awesome!"

So I got louder. "Hey! Hey! Where am I? Where is this? Who are you? How do I get out of here? Where is the door?"

Amazingly, he stopped talking and came over to me.

He said quite calmly, "Nowat."

"Yes," I said a little more calmly. "That's a good question. Now what?"

"Nowat."

"Okay, I agree. What do we do now?"

"Nowat."

I just stared at him.

"Dude, my moniker is, like, Nowat. One word. Nowat. If you want, we can, like, also do a few rounds of who's like, on first."

Then I caught on.

Sometimes it takes me a while.

"Okay, Now What…"

"Nowat, please. One word. I am not a Now What. I am Nowat."

"Okay, okay…ah…Nowat. at the risk of being on first, now what…or maybe what now?

"Isn't this, like, magnificent?" he asked.

"I guess. But where are we? How do we get out of here? The door is gone!"

He looked at me and calmly offered, "Don't worry. I have, like, been here before. I know the way out. It is through."

"Through? Through what? There's no door! Not even a window!"

"We go through what we're, like, supposed to go through."

"But there's nothing here to, ah, like, go through."

Then I noticed a small, dark rectangle, some distance away off to my left.

"What is that?" I asked, pointing.

Nowat turned around and looked at the rectangle.

"I don't know. Why don't we, like, go see?"

So we did.

***

It took us some time to get to the rectangle. It was further away than I first thought. But when you have no frame of reference, it's all white, I guess anything can be as close or as far away as it wants if there's nothing else around. Maybe that's physics.

Anyway, as we closed in on the rectangle, I could see that it was a giant copy of one of my paintings that I had done last year. It was at least five feet wide and seven feet tall. It stood all by itself—no framing, no bracing, no nothing. And there were no shadows around or on it—a great gallery hanging.

I stood in front of it dumbfounded.

After a few minutes, I finally said to Nowat, "What is this doing here?" Brilliant question.

He said nothing. He just stared.

Then I decided to check out the back of the painting. I walked around it and there was another of my paintings on the back. I continued around to the front to tell Nowat what I had found, but there was now a new painting on the front. It wasn't the first one I saw. But it was one of mine.

"What is this?" I asked nobody in particular.

After a hesitation, Nowat replied, "I believe it is, like, your mindeye… your inventory."

"My mindeye?"

"Yes."

"I didn't know I had one."

"Everybody has one."

"Aw, come on! I've never heard that."

"It is usually, like, called memory, but sometimes it gets organized so you can see you."

"So you can see you."

"No, so *you* can see you. Not me."

"Okay, so I have memories. I have a mindeye. What else did you call it?"

"An inventory. Mindeyes, or inventories are, like, organized memories. In this case, it appears to be, like, your painting mindeye."

"So what good is it? So I have organized memories…ah, a painting mindeye."

"Nothing."

"Nothing?"

"Nothing."

He just sat there, staring at me.

Then it hit me.

Nothing.

Nothing was what Videre talked about.

Videre was an old blind lady who had helped me discover the qualities of nothing. Videre, her dog Cy, a gentleman called Theodore, and an old dragon named Fumie had led me through the series of charmed blue door experiences that had given direction to my art…and life.

That's what this was about—*more nothing*!

"Did Videre send you?" I asked cautiously.

His face lit up. "Ah…the, like, surely righteous lady. She might have, like, suggested that I make your acquaintance."

"So, you're another of Videre's friends, come to fix me?"

"Do you need, like, fixing?"

"No I don't need…like, fixing!"

"But you are…like…deviating."

"Deviating?"

"Deviating."

"You say I'm deviating."

"Okay."

"What business is it of yours if I'm, ah, deviating…or not? Anyway, what are you doing with my mindeye, or memories, or whatever you call it? It's no business of yours. And, besides that, I am not a deviator, whatever that is."

"Ah, but it is, like, my business," replied Nowat with a twinkle in his eye.

"But I don't know you. Besides, my paintings, my memories, and my so-called deviations are mine. How I paint and what I paint is my business and *only* my business!"

"But other people have to, like, look at your paintings. I'm other people. That makes it, like, my business."

"What are you, some kind of painters' police?"

"No."

"Hey, if somebody doesn't appreciate my art, that's no skin off my back. I'm not going to change how or what I do what I do for you or anybody."

"Like, okay."

"Okay?"

"Okay."

"So, if I could be so bold, what *do* you want here?"

"Nothing."

"Nothing?"

"Sometimes…it's, like, good to let someone else see your mindeye so, like, you can see you better."

"So you get to see my mindeye… ah, inventory, so I can see me better."

"Like, cool."

"How does that work, if I may be so bold as to ask?"

"I don't know."

"You don't know."

"But it works, like, darn good."

"Well, I guess I can't get out of here until we get…through this, so let's, ah, deviate through my inventory."

***

We started walking around the painting rectangle. Each time we got to the other side a different painting was revealed. But I found that if I went back the other way around the rectangle, the prior paintings came back. It was like pages in a book. I could go forward and I could go back. As the real painting size changed, so did the rectangle.

Magic…or not?

I really didn't want to admit to Nowat that I was struggling with a problem. I had been told to produce a more consistent body of work. That's what people like. It's more saleable, I guess.

Consistency. I really don't know what that means. After all, I'm the painter painting what I paint in my "style," whatever that is. Do I paint the same painting over and over to be consistent? Do I paint the same subject over and over? Just what is it? Ultimately, I guess the question is all about what I choose to paint.

So on we went, round and round the rectangle.

After seeing a large portion of my paintings, it struck me.

I said to Nowat, "I see what you mean. Maybe I am, ah, deviating."

"What do you mean?"

"Hey! You said I was deviating. You should know what that means."

"I know, like, what I mean. But what you mean can be different. Besides, it's like your mindeye, not mine."

"Okay…I guess. Seeing everything together like this helps. There's just a lot of different things here—some realistic, some abstract, some dark, some light, some political, some blah, some successful, some not so successful."

"Leaving out the, like, *successful* and the *not so* judgements, what is there?"

"It *varies*. I like that word varies better."

"Okay. Is varies what you want?"

"It's what's there—not what I would call the desirable consistent body of work."

"What's that?"

"You can't have realistic and abstract work all together…right?"

"Why not?"

"Because."

"Says who?"

"I don't know. That's just what I've been told."

"And you believe everything you're, like, told? How do you feel about that?"

"How do I feel about what?"

"Yes. How do you feel about being consistent?"

"I don't know about feeling. I know about thinking."

"Who, like, cares about your thinking?"

"Huh?"

We both got silent and continued looking at paintings.

***

We walked around my paintings for quite a while—sometimes I stopped and commented on what I saw. Nowat said nothing in response.

I had noticed that the paintings kept getting larger and larger, in keeping with the increased size and proportion of the real paintings. After looking at a large piece—a 12 foot by 48 foot monster—the longest I had ever done, I said, "This is probably the last one."

"Then, we are, like, through."

"Well, I hate to say it, but maybe this was a good exercise," I said.

"Yes."

"I still don't know how I feel about my varying…or deviating, but I know I am. How do I know if that's okay or not?"

"Don't worry. You will be contacted."

"Huh?"

"That's how you get to know you. You will, like, feel it. And that will become clear. But, like, for now, knowing where you are can help get you where you want to be."

"So, I know where I are, or am, and that will help me knowing me."

"Like, yeah! You got it! Now, let's, like get out of here."

"Sure."

***

Before continuing with this story, dear reader, I offer you the chance to review my painting mindeye, or inventory. The mindeye only contains last year's paintings. I would probably be even more confused if it were over a longer time span.

The following pages contain photos of all the paintings in my mindeye. As you will see, they do…vary a bit.

You may use your own criterion in judging the works.

But whatever criterion you use, make sure you ask yourself how you *feel* about them.

Note: All of the paintings which follow were accomplished by Jim Brock. They are of watercolor on gessoed hardboard or on clay covered hardboard. The single exception is painting 1248101 which is watercolor on gallery wrapped canvas.

The numbers in front of the paintings' names indicate the painting size as well as the sequence number accomplished in that size. For example, painting 5711 is 5 inches by 7 inches, and is number 1 in series 1.

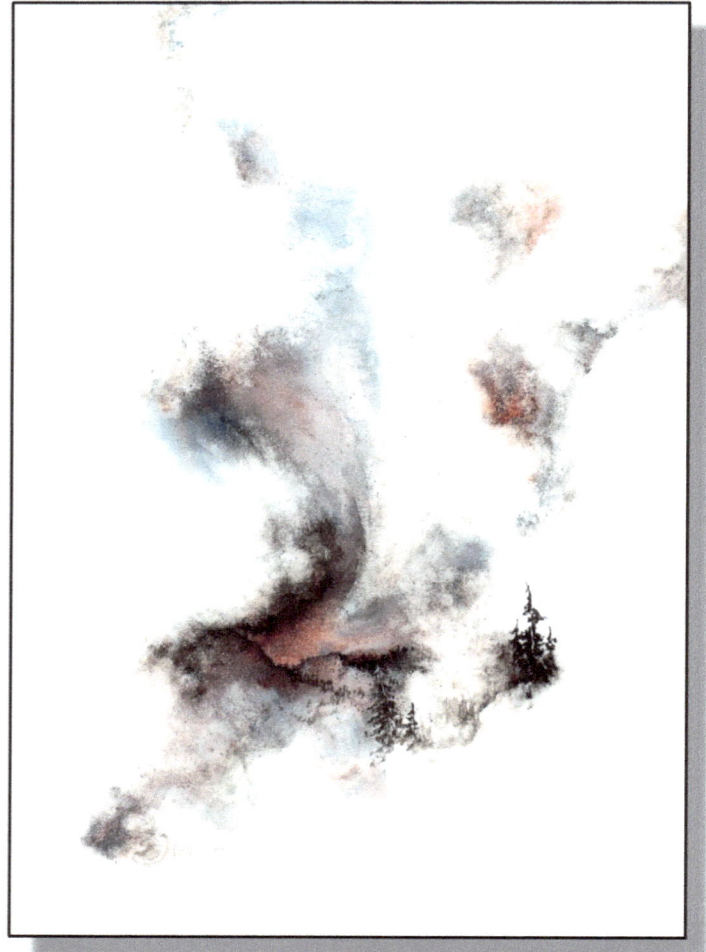

5711 Sunrise

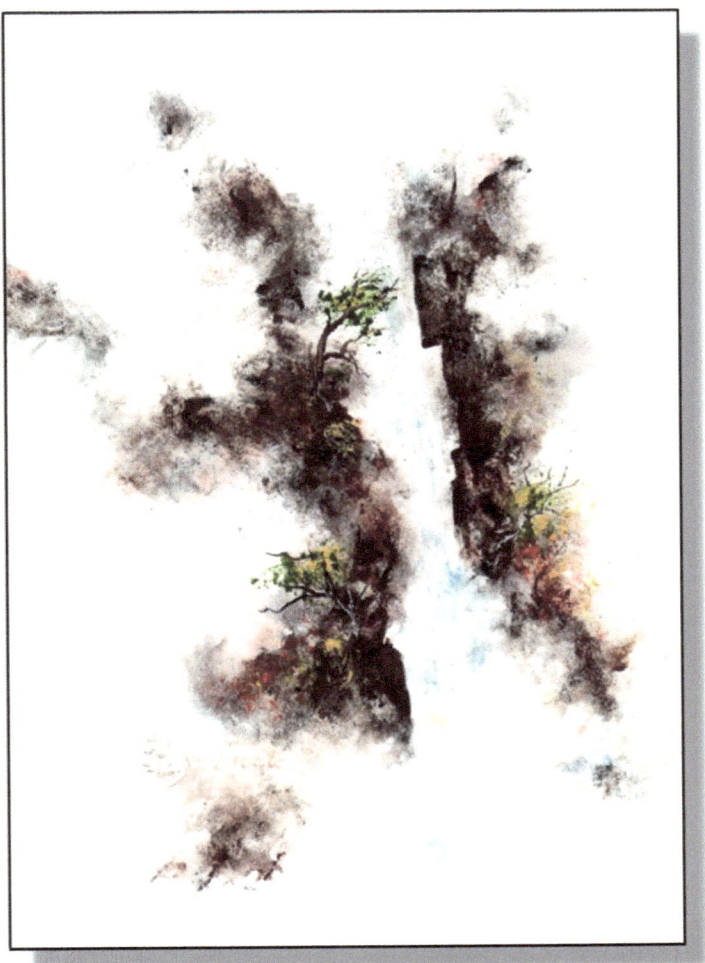

5712 Falls

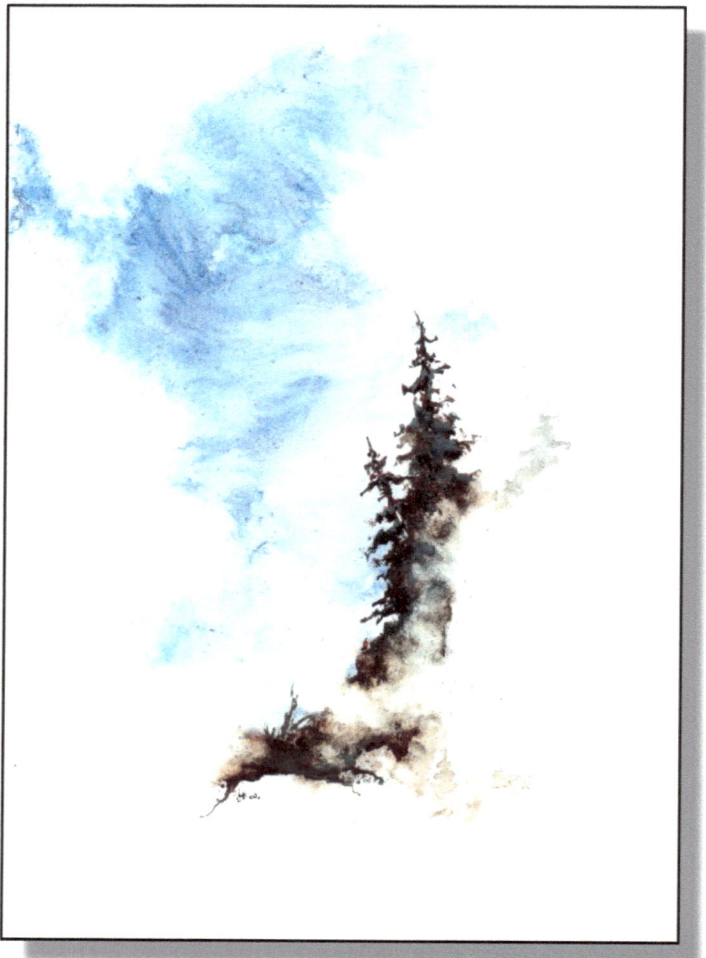

5713 Uphill

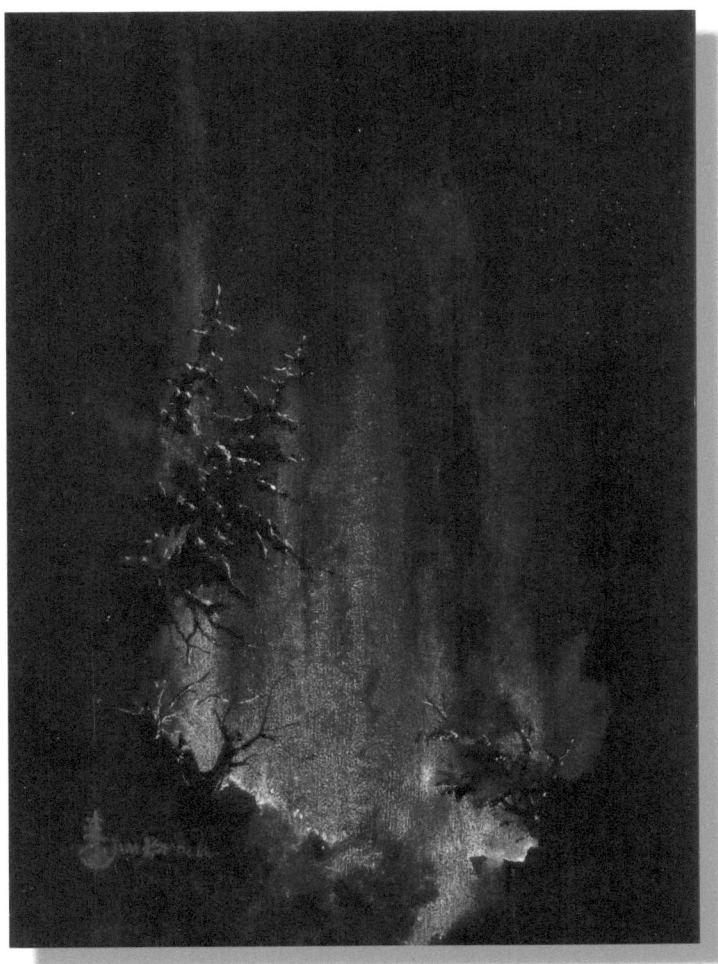

5714 Night Falls

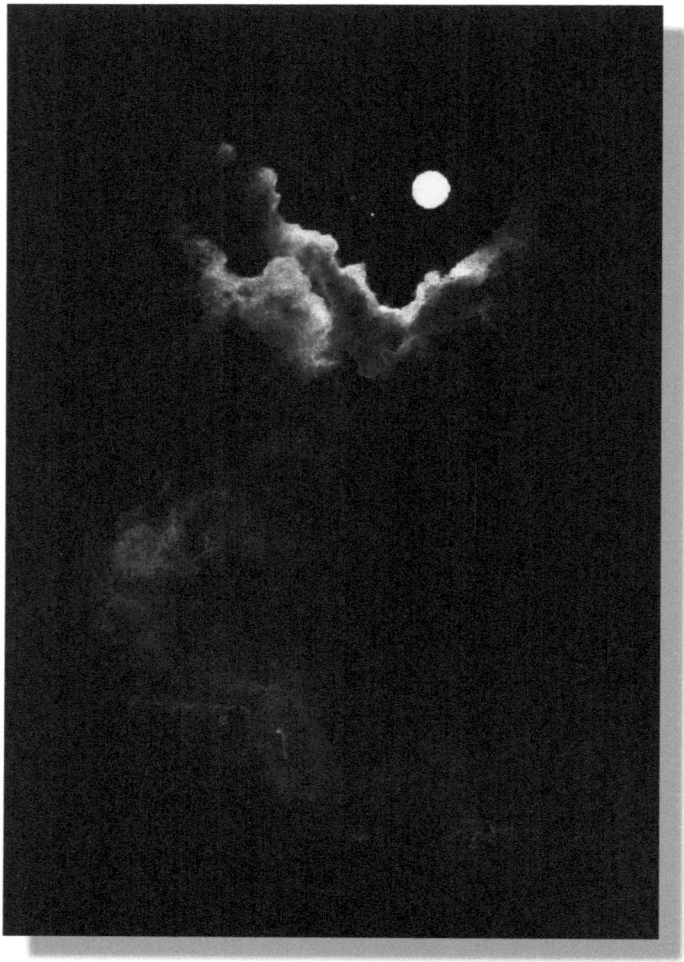

5715 Reflections

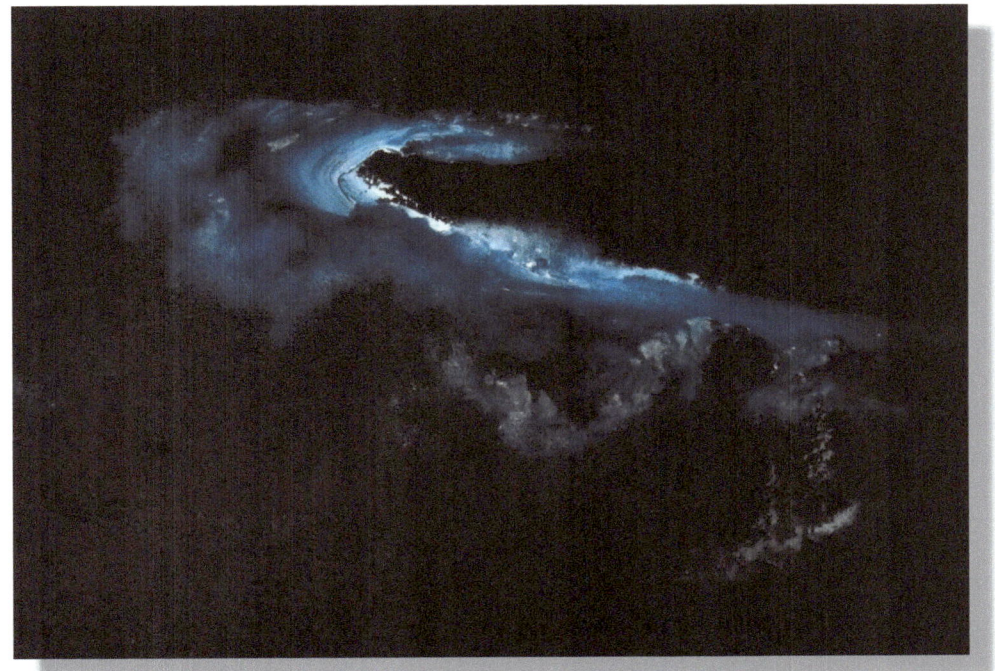

5716 Night Blue

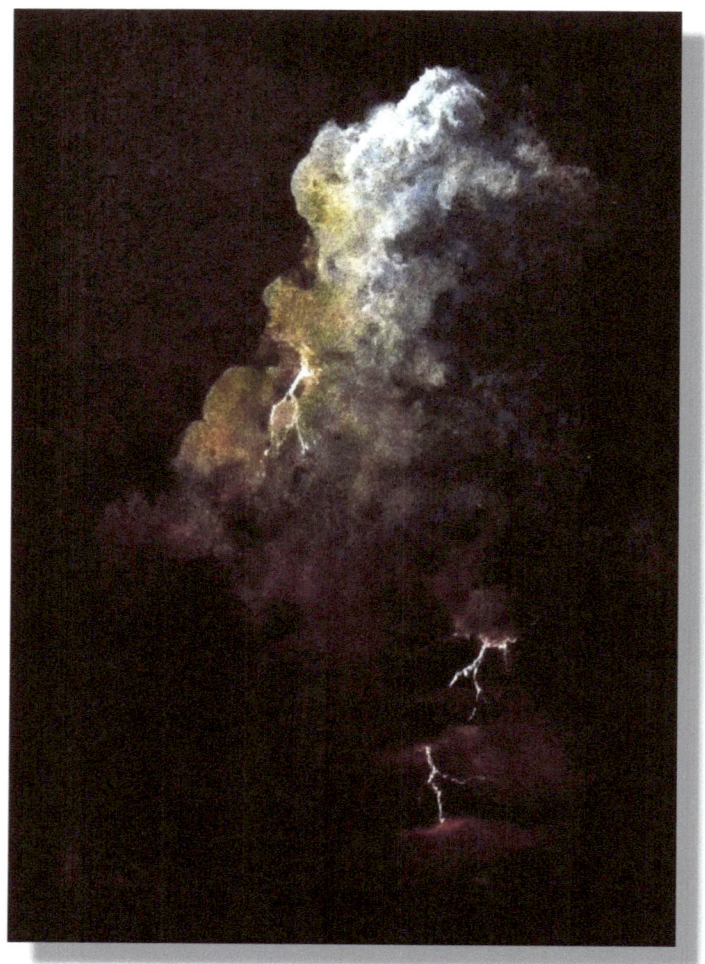

5717 Evening Thunder

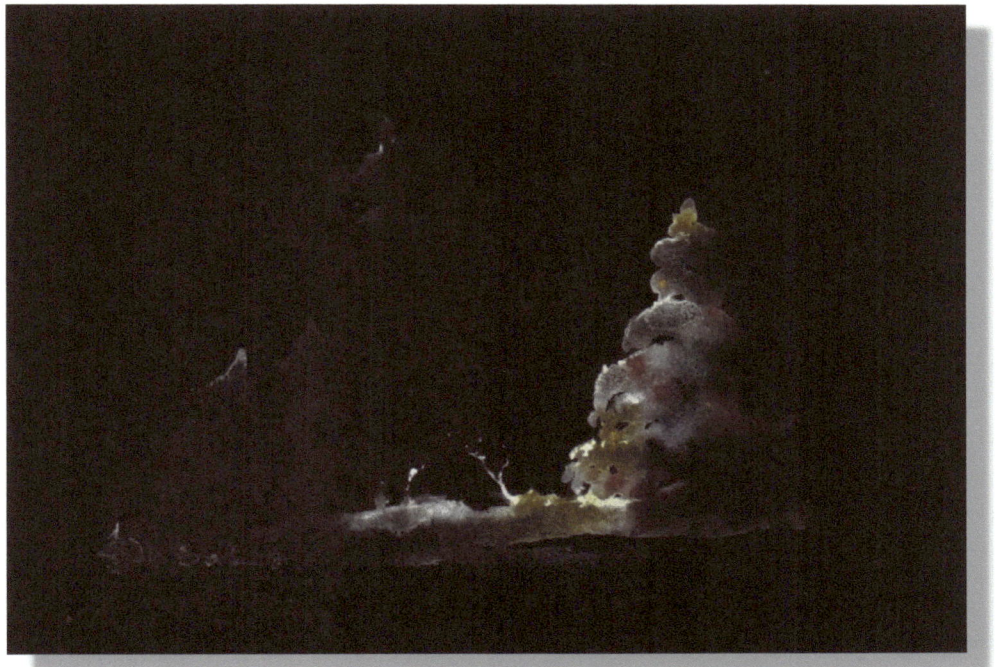

5718 Forest Christmas

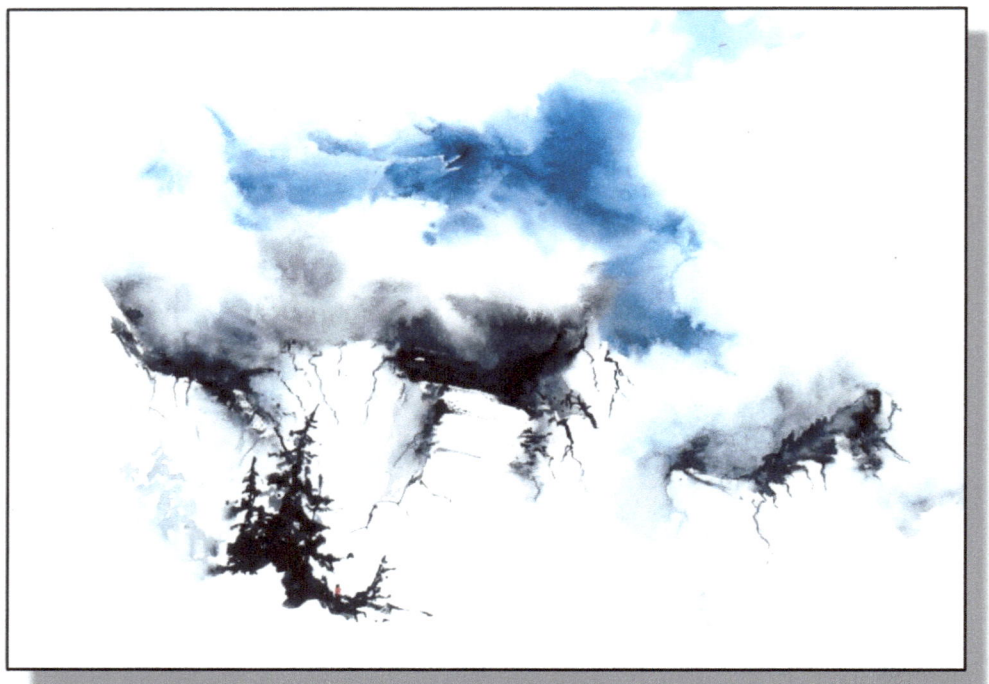

5719 Ridges

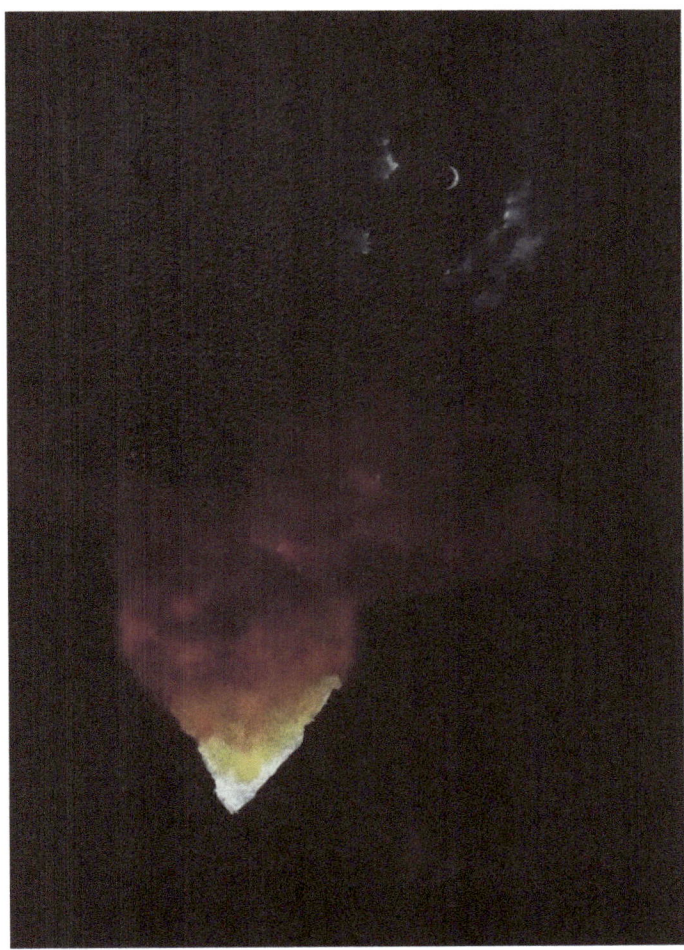

57110 Desert Sunrise

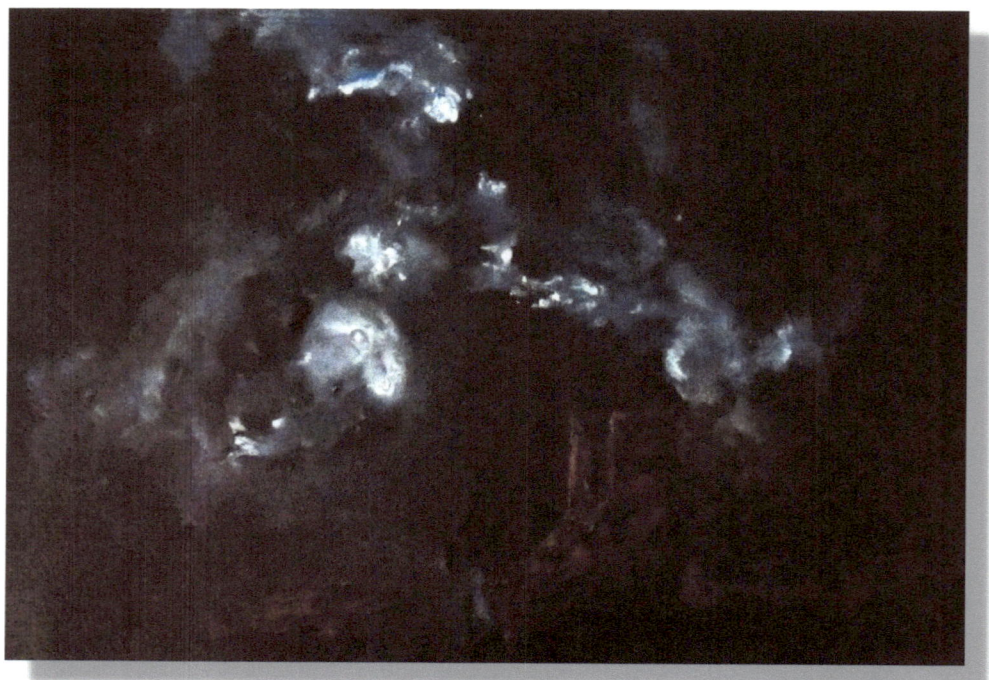

57111 Desert Storm

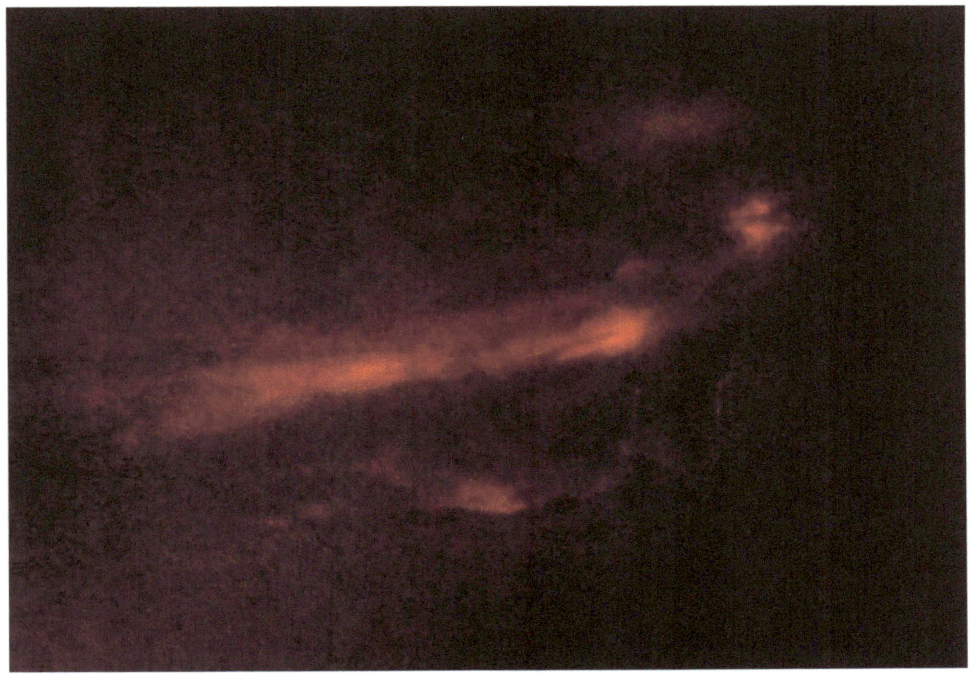

57112 Desert Evening

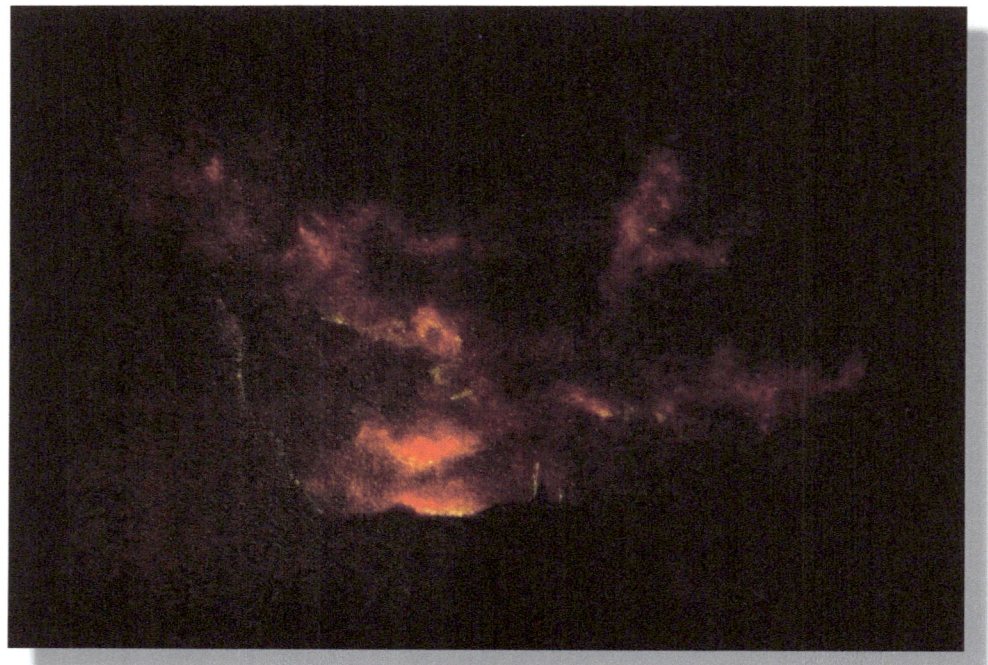

57113 Sunset

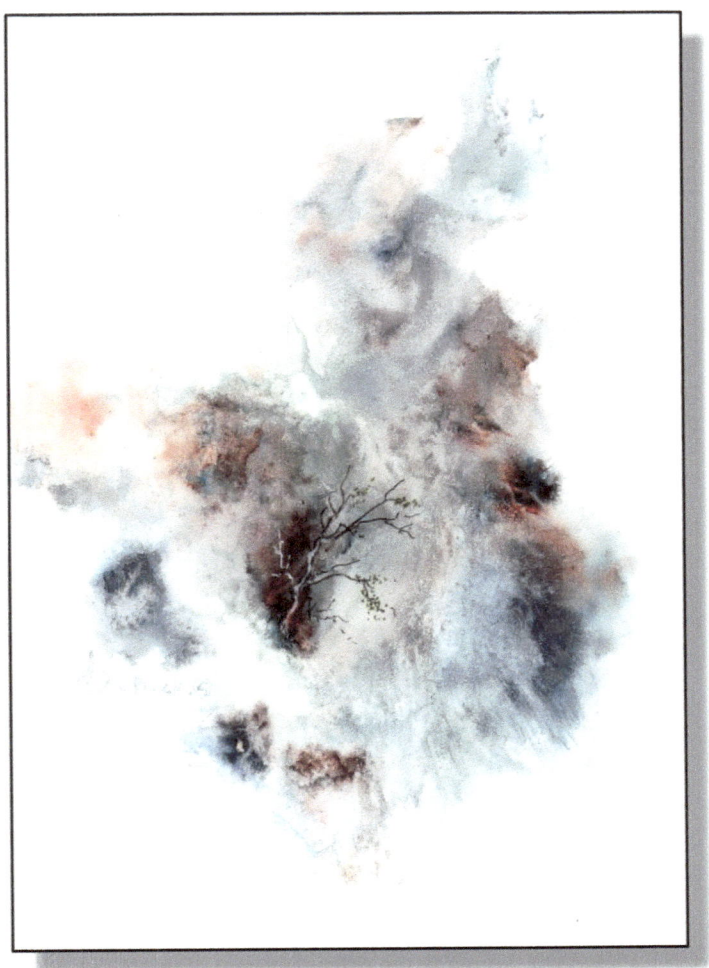

57114 Solitude

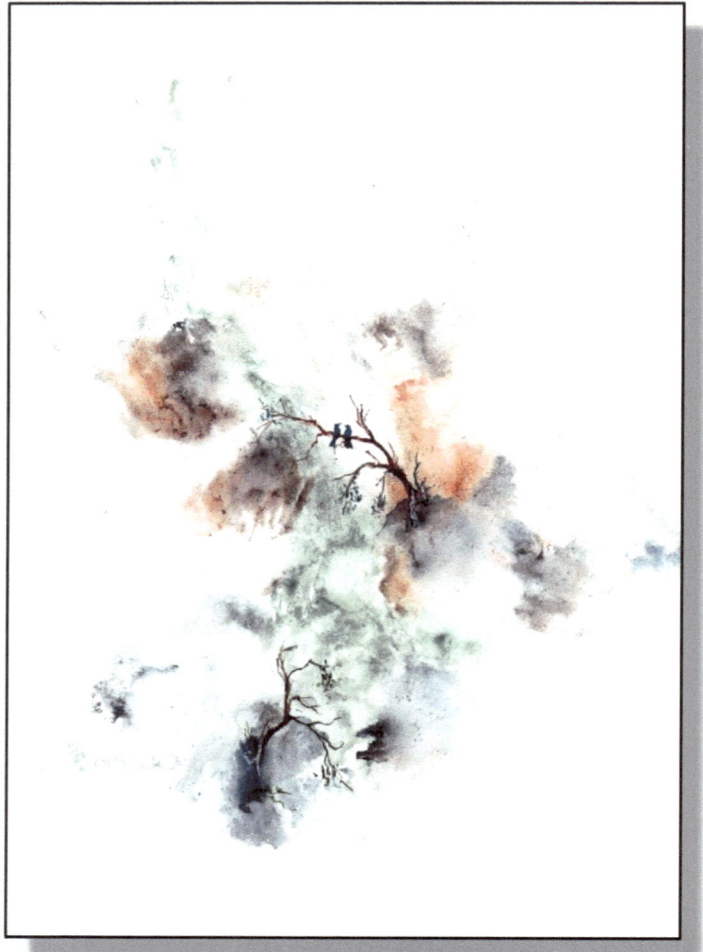

57115 Blue Company

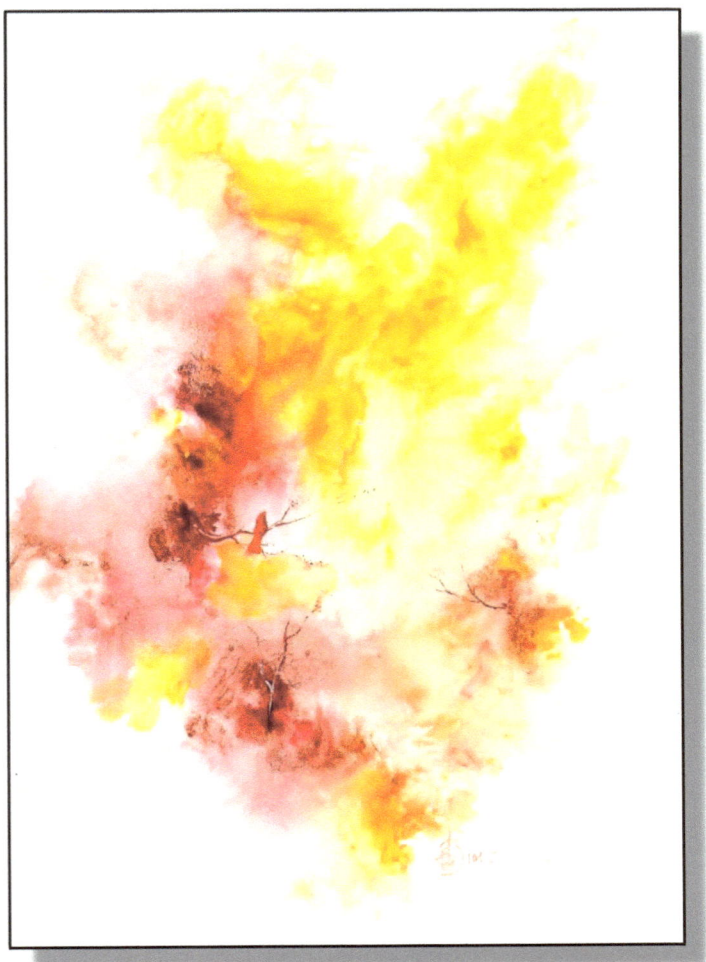

57116 Red Reflections

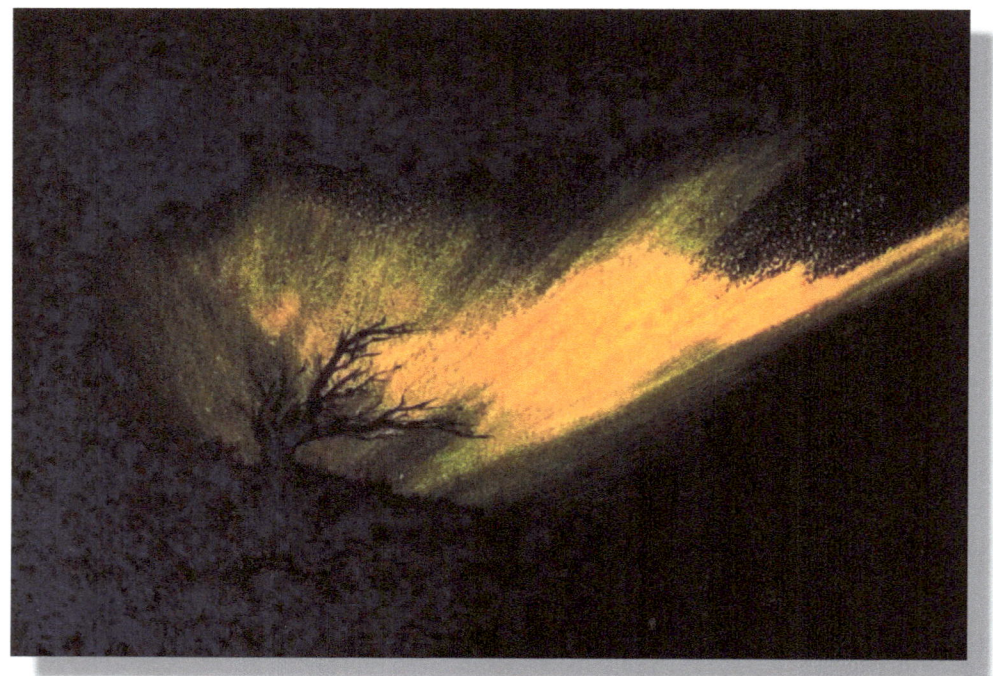

57117 Aurora

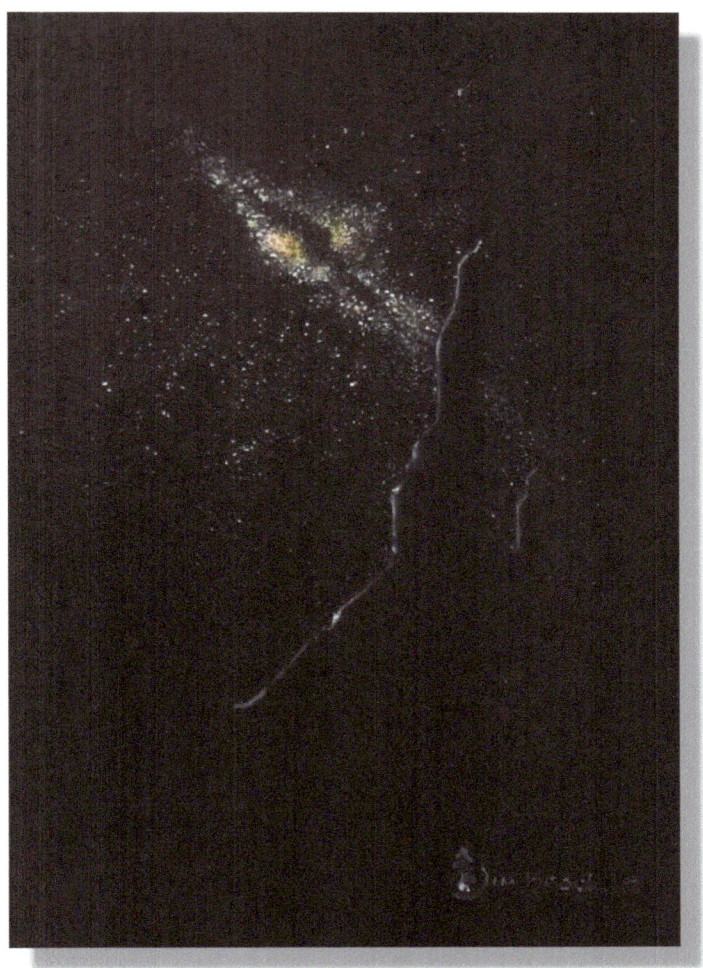

57118 Desert Sky

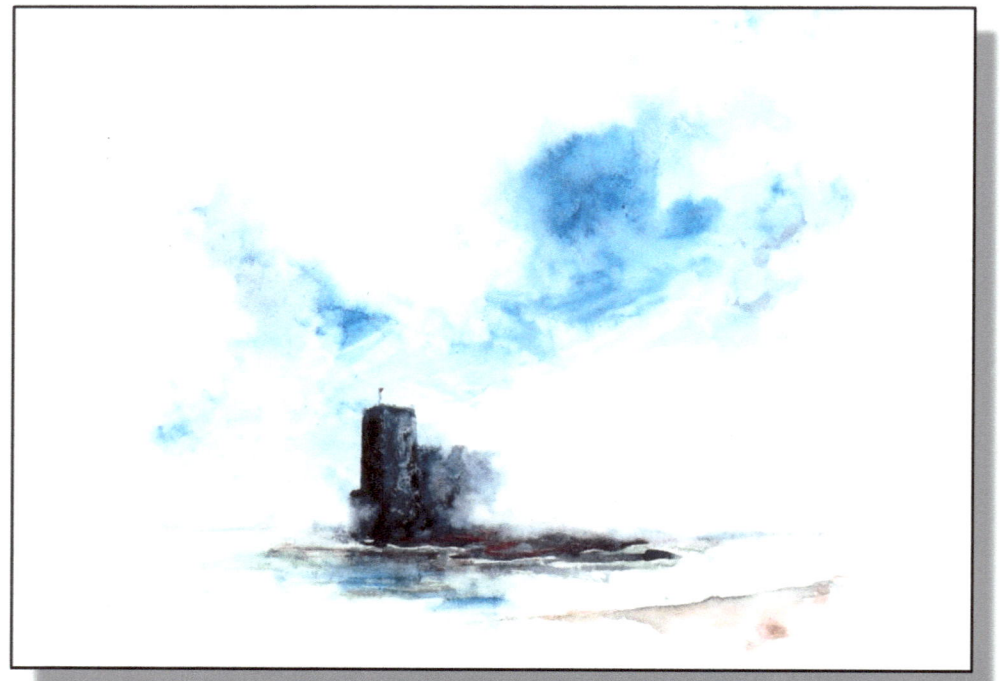

57119 Castle

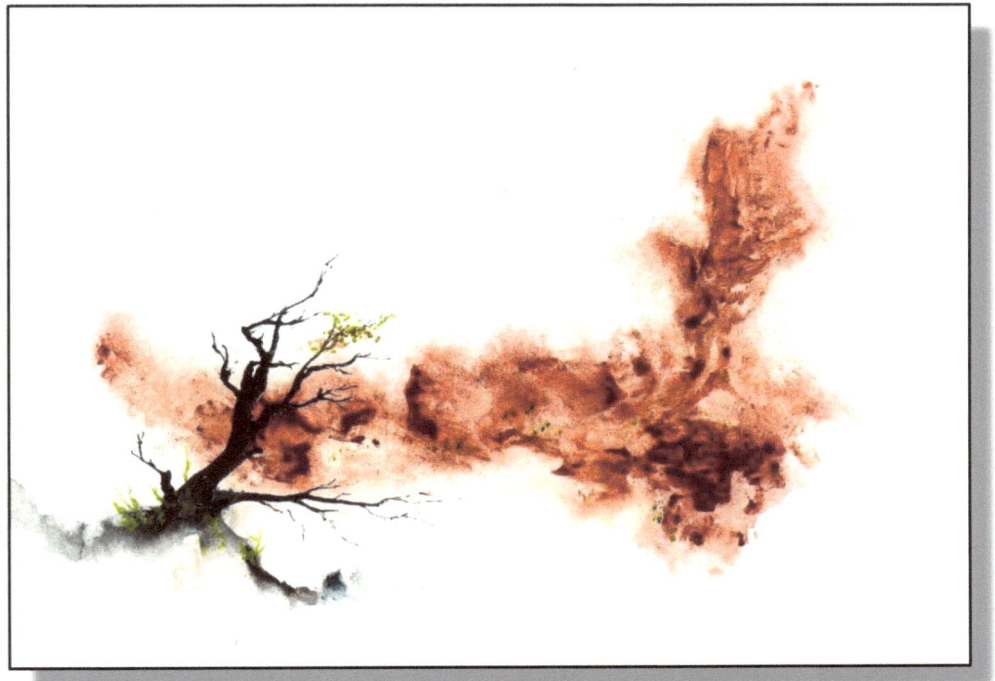

57120 Drought

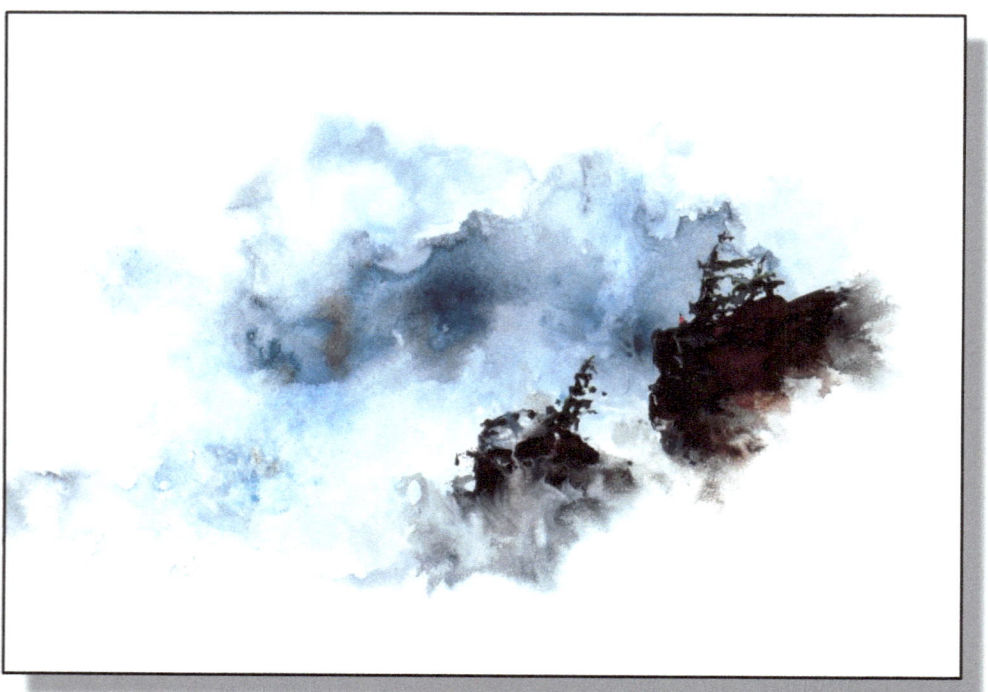

57121 Shore Wind

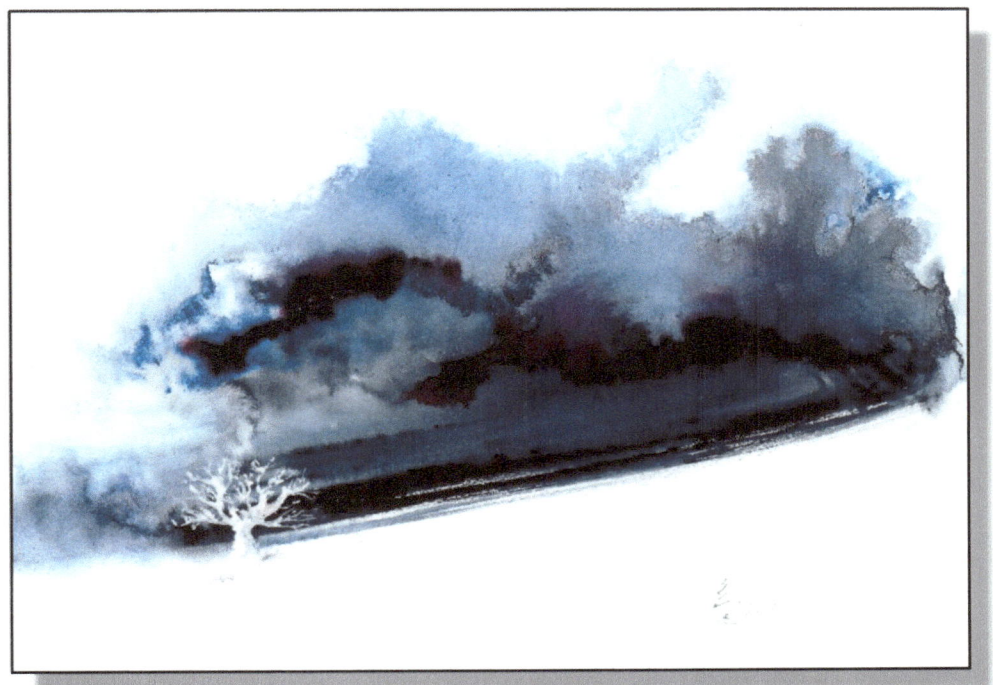

57122 Comes Winter

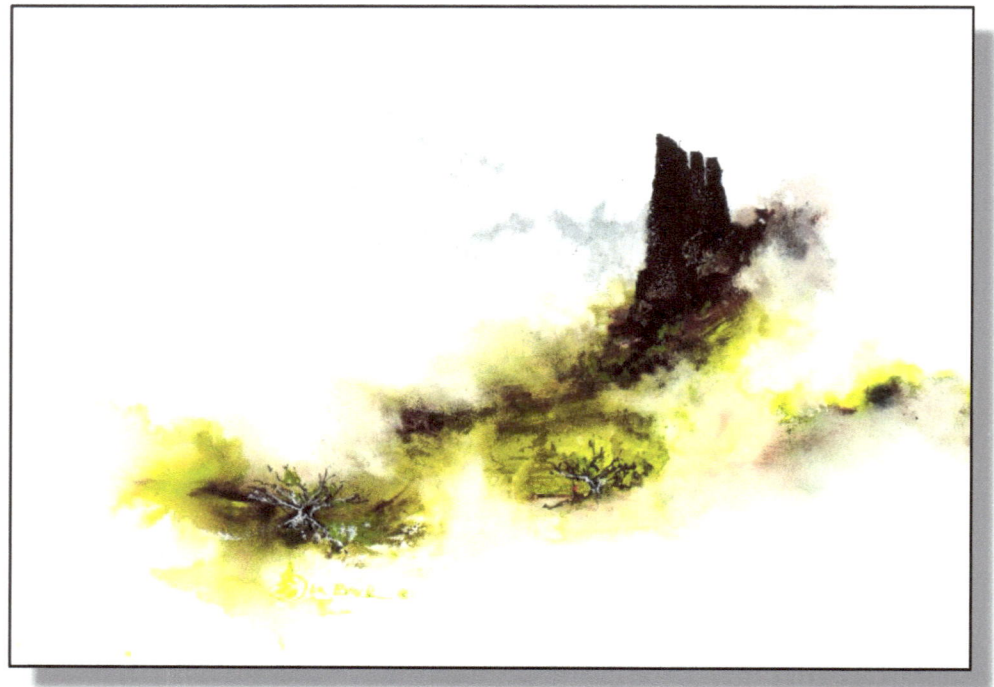

57123 Monument

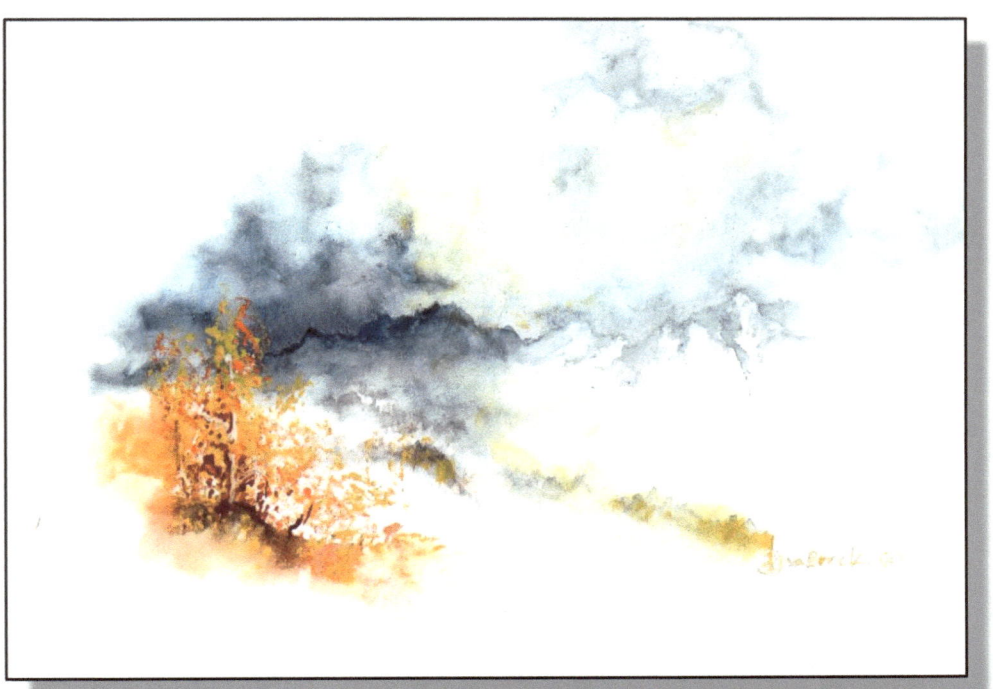

57124 Coming Storm

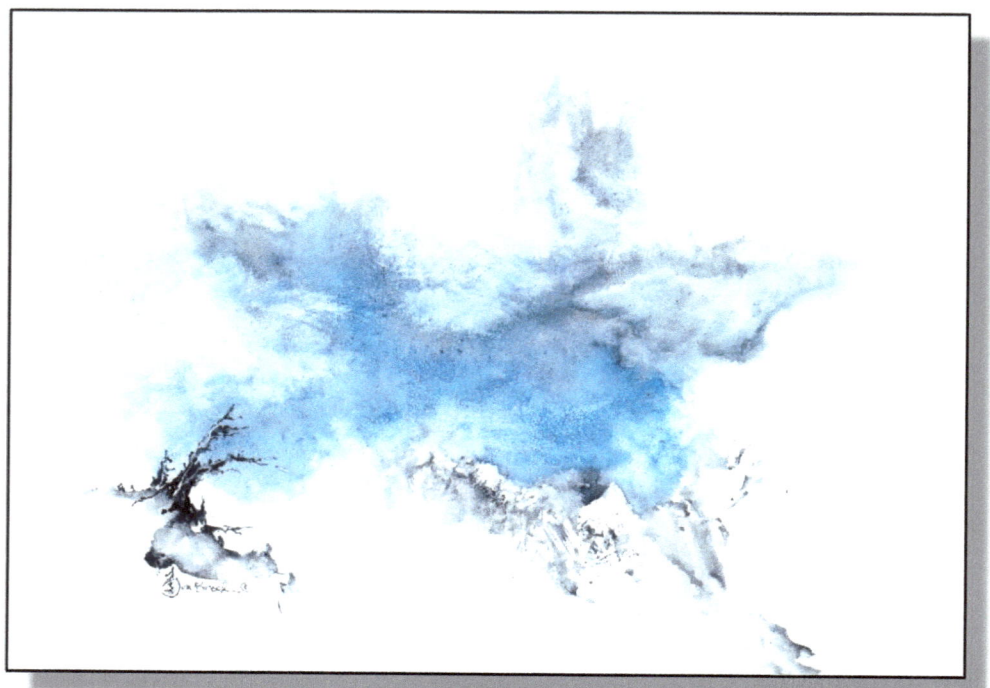

57125 Mountain Ridge

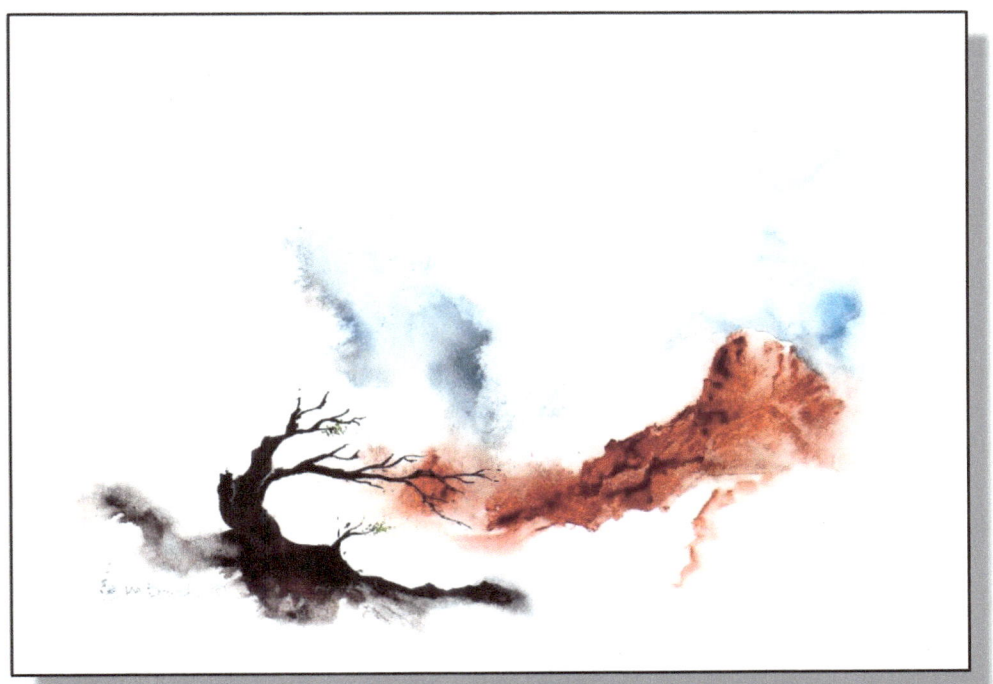

57126 Desert Point

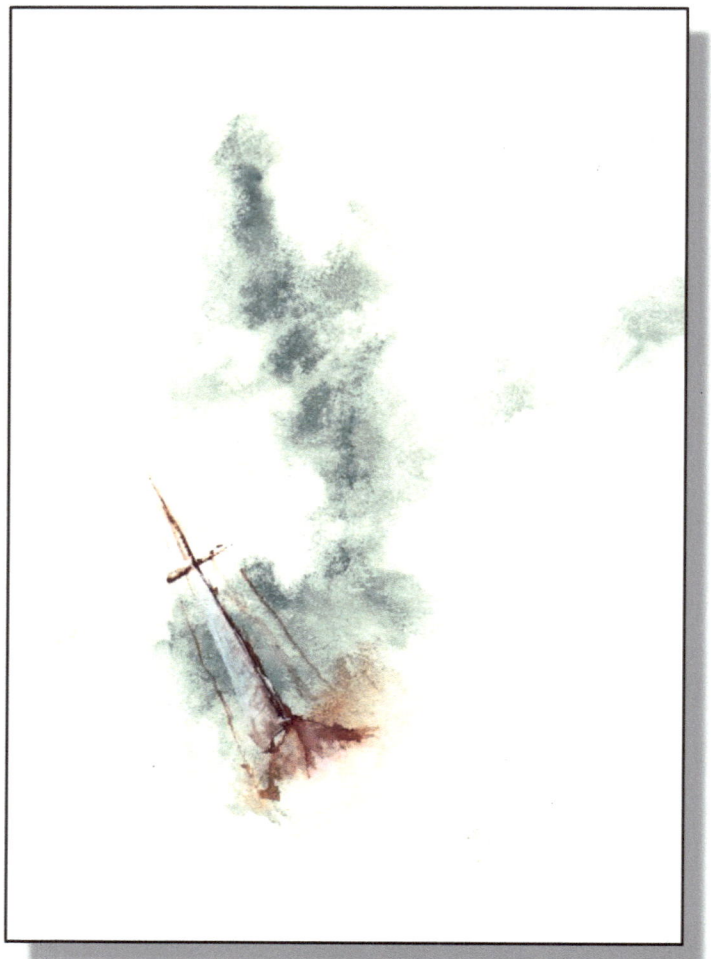

57127 Sailing

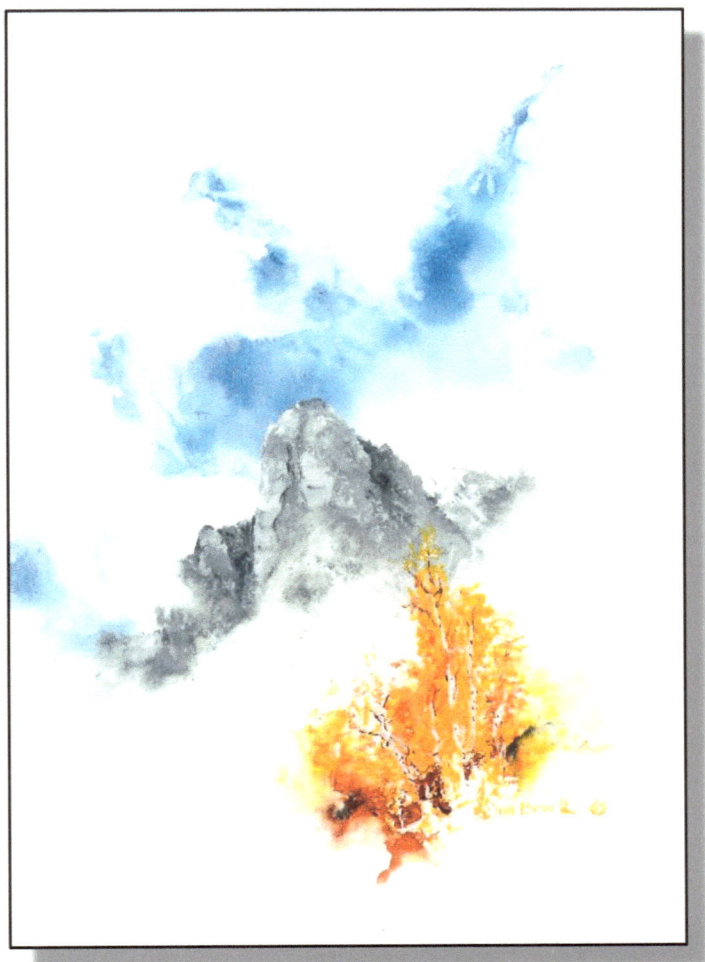

57128 Fall

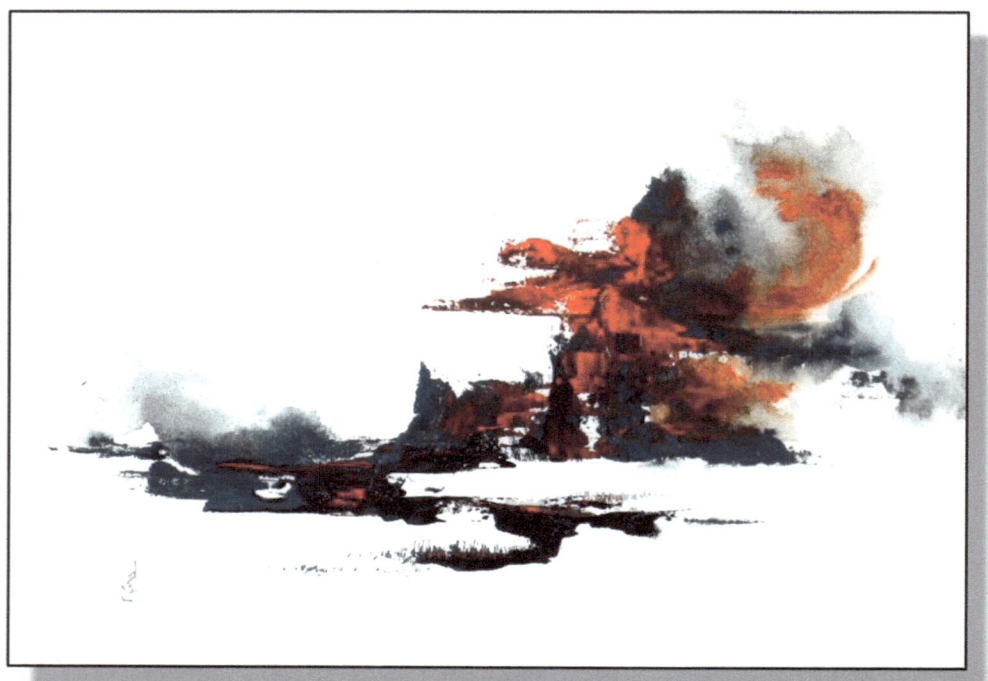

57129 Ridges

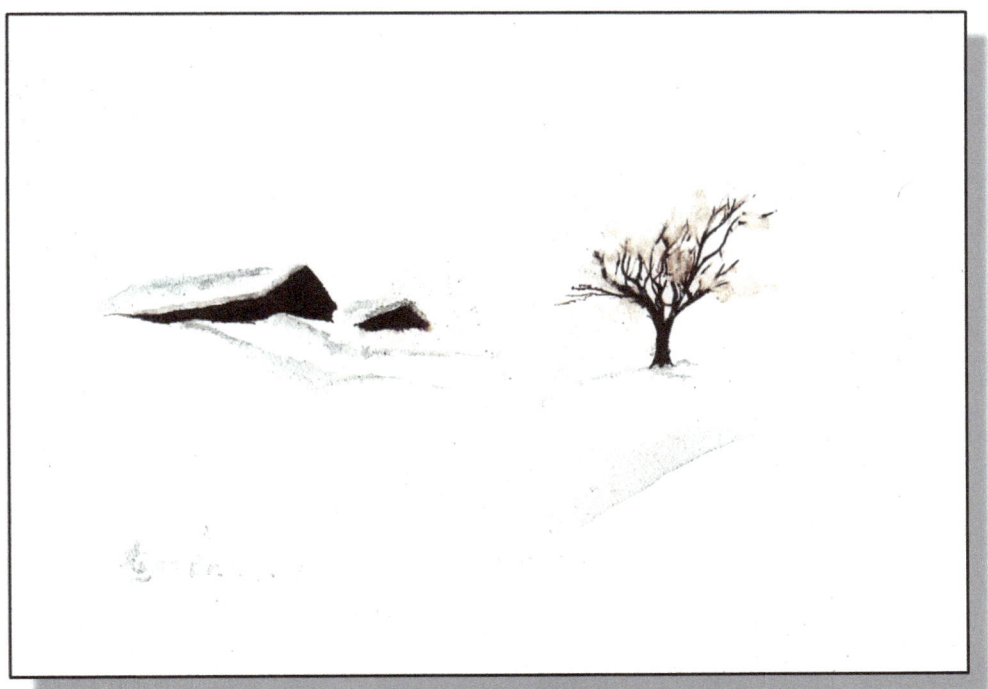

57130 Winterscape

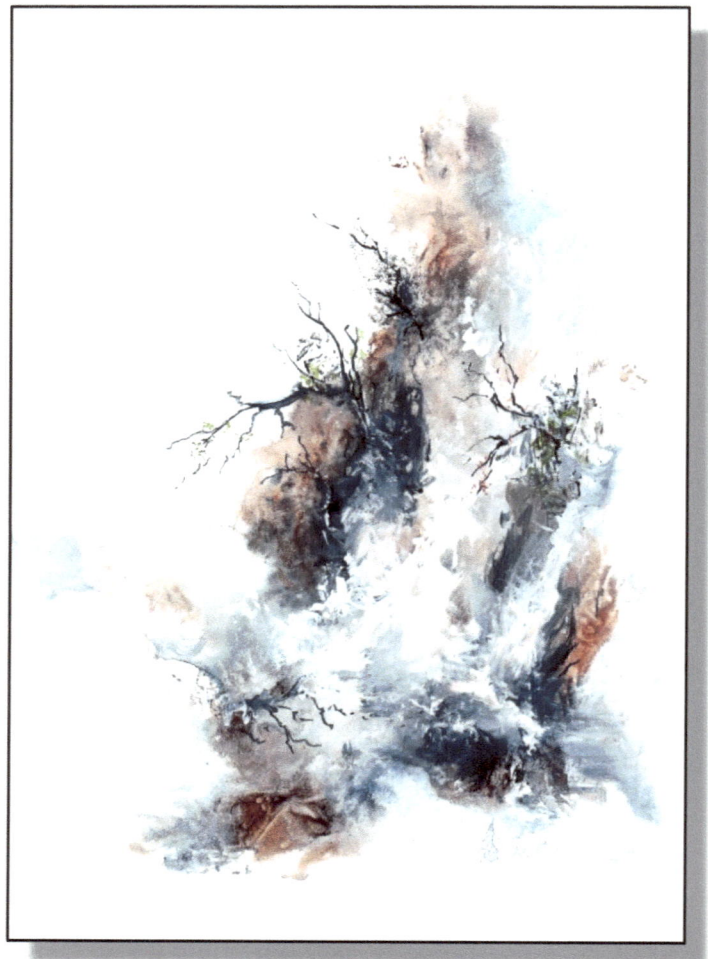

57131 Splash

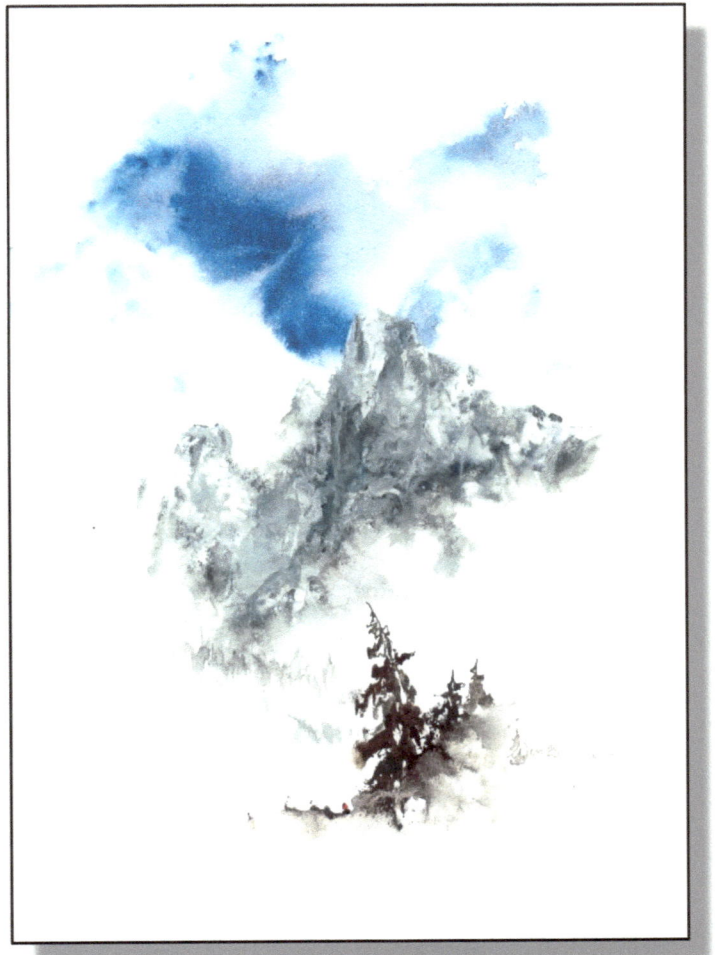

57132 Ridge View

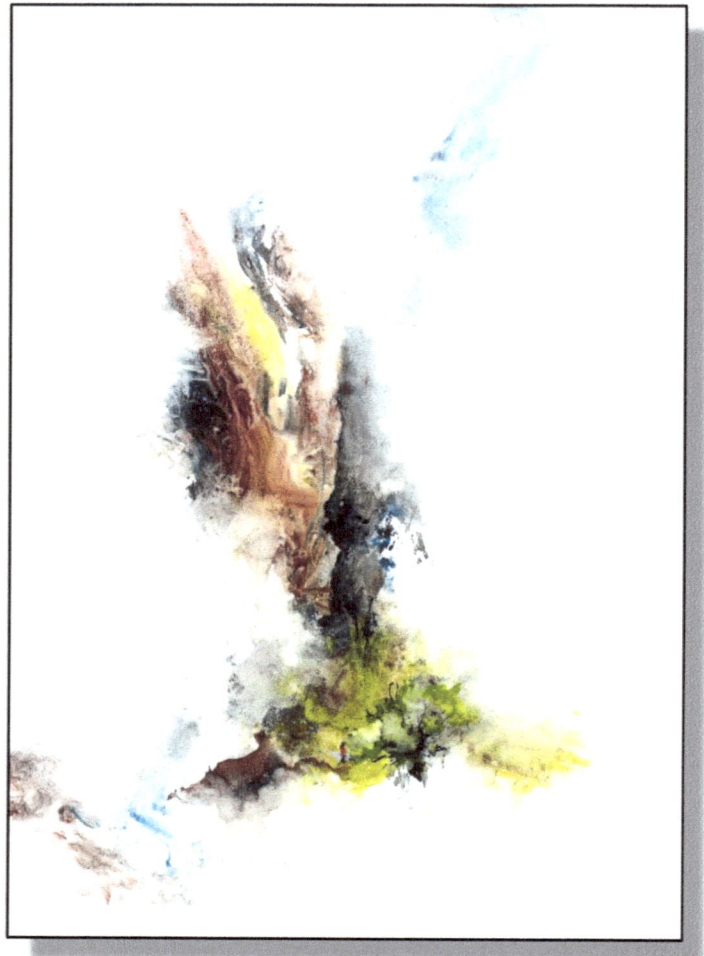

57133 Into the Golden Valley

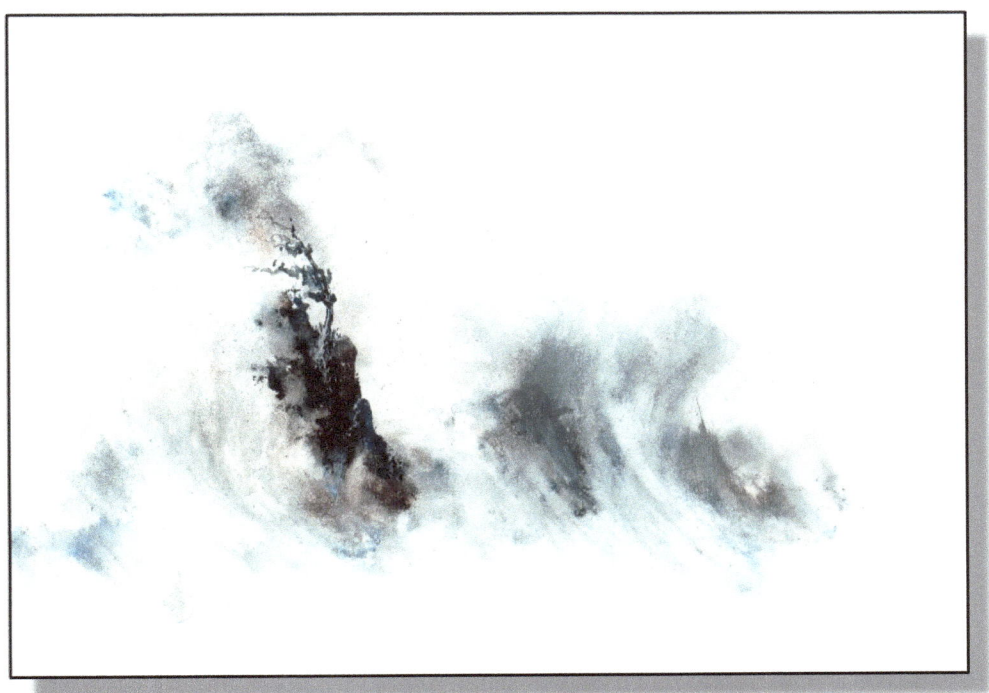

57134 Blown

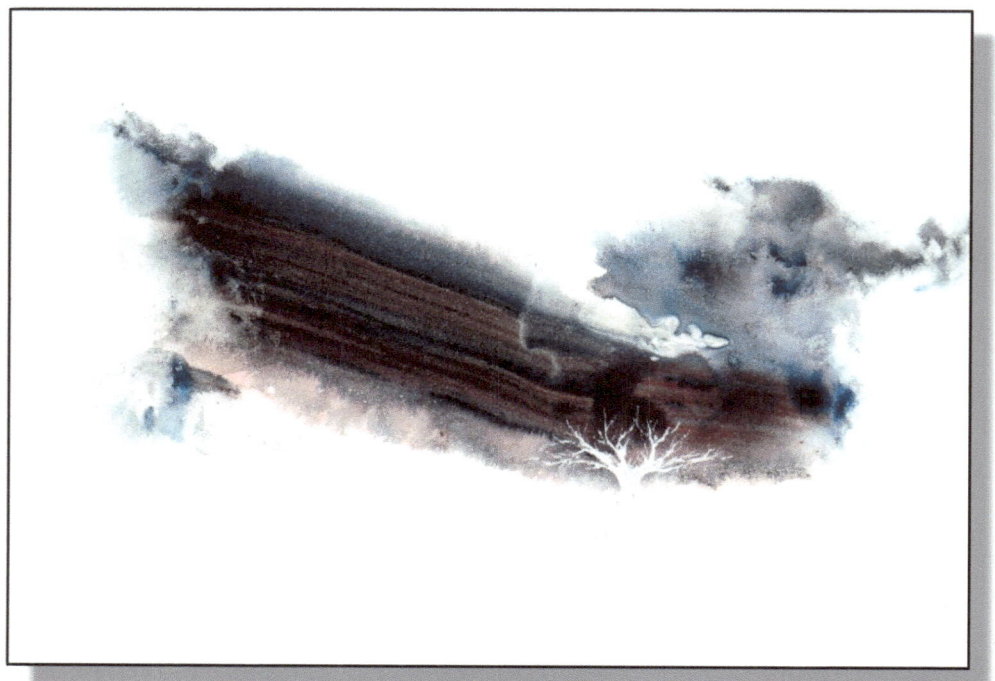

57135 Winter

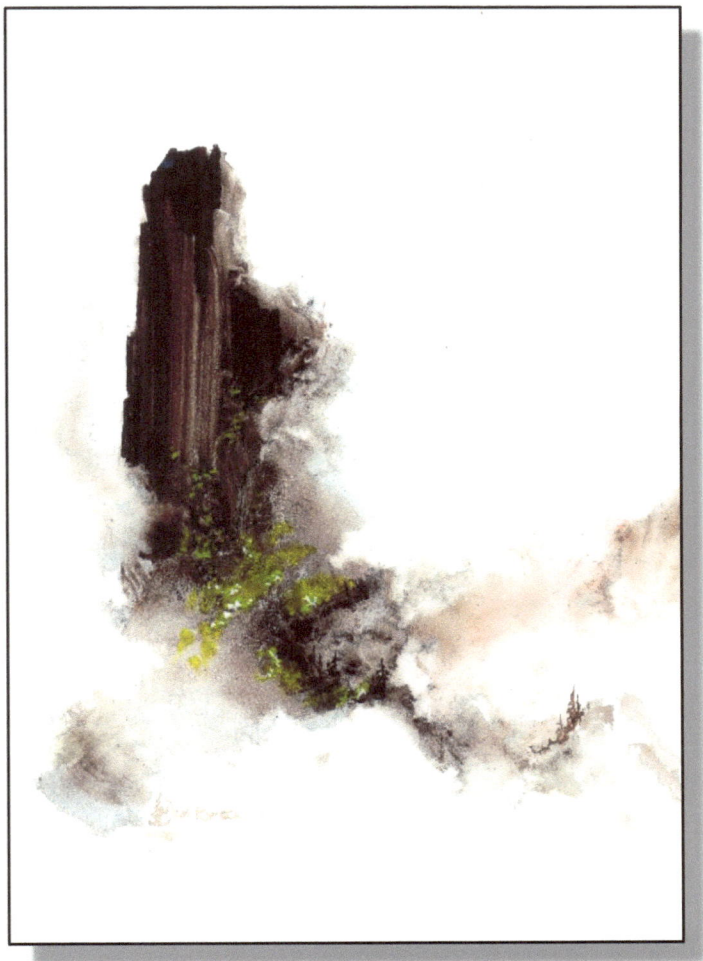

57136 Up & Down

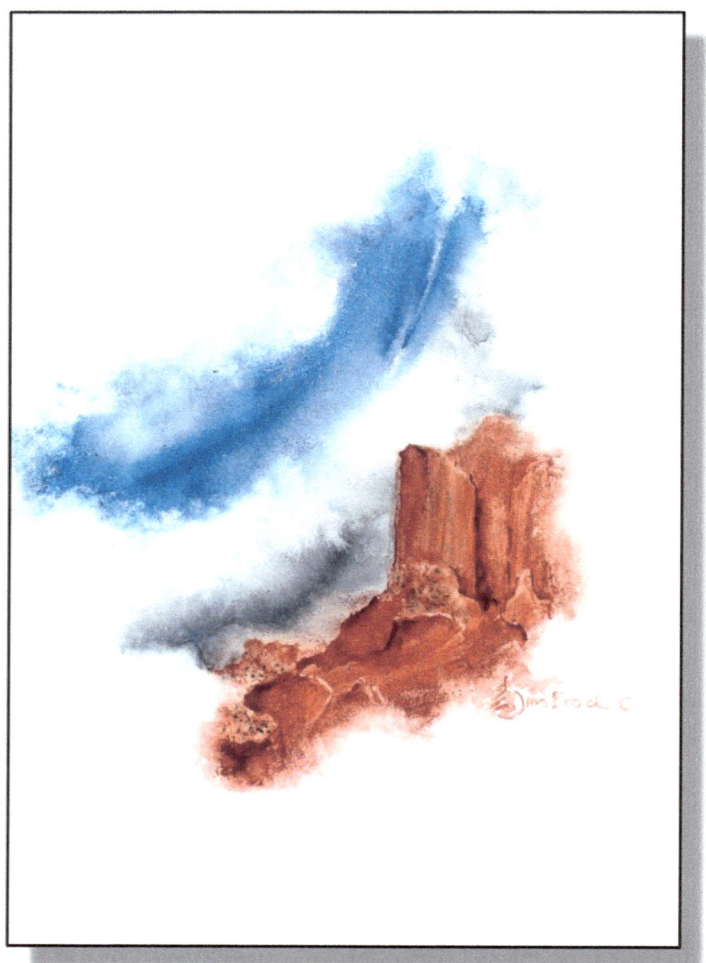

57137 Desert Wall

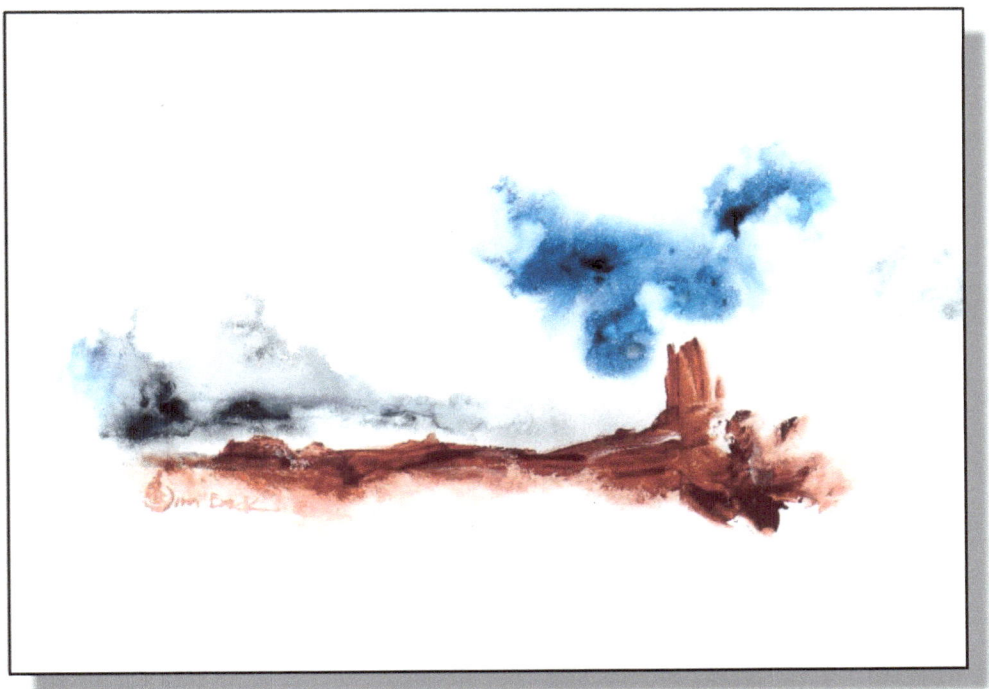

57138 Desert Ridge

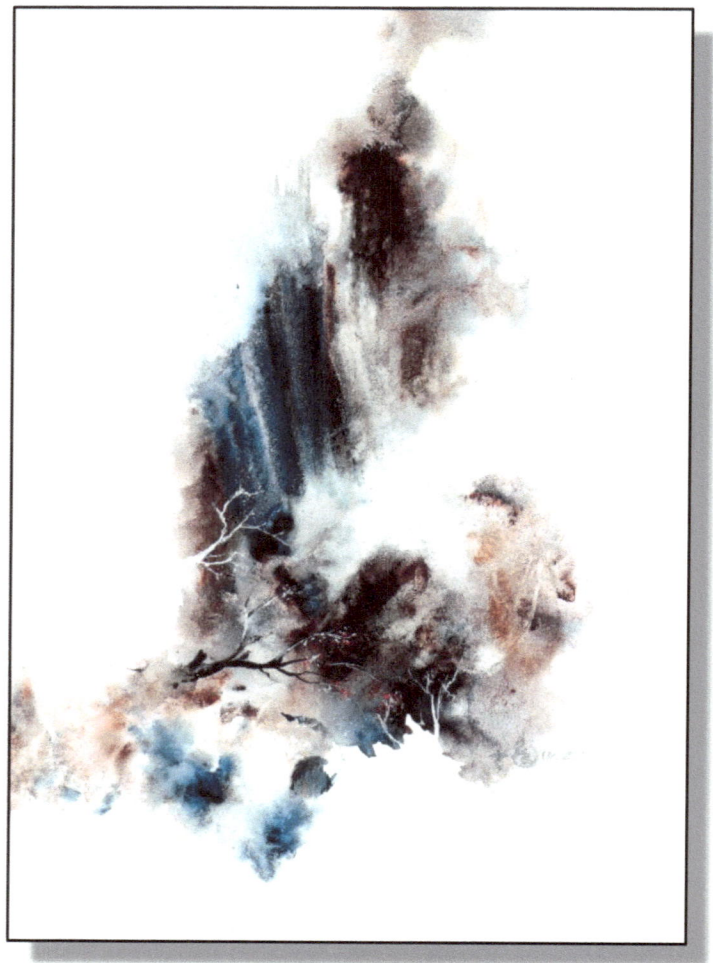

57139 Falls

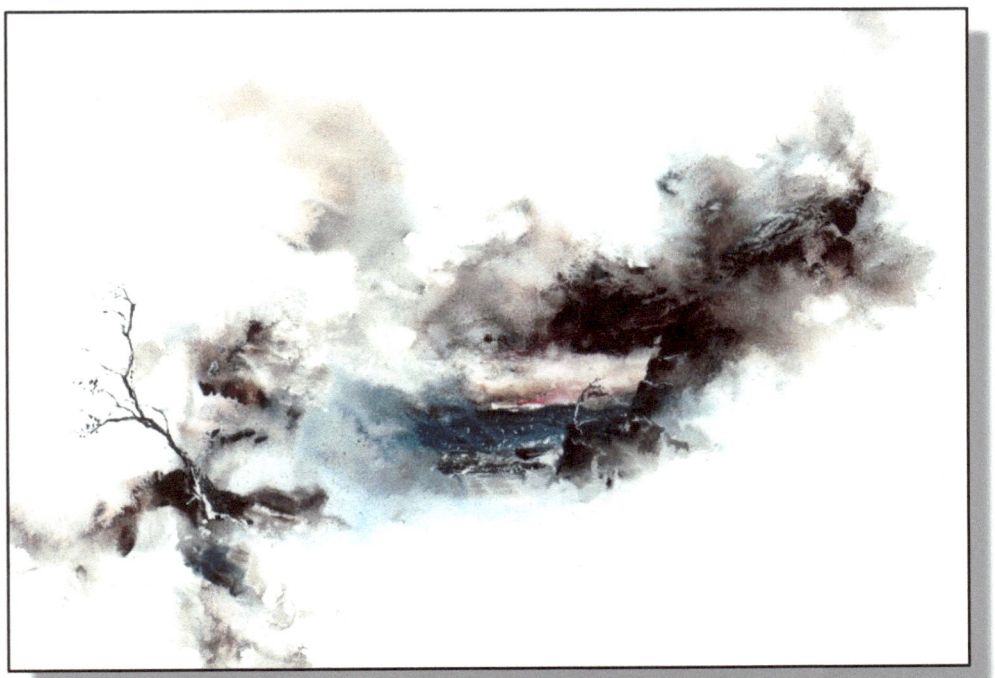

57140 Windy Coast

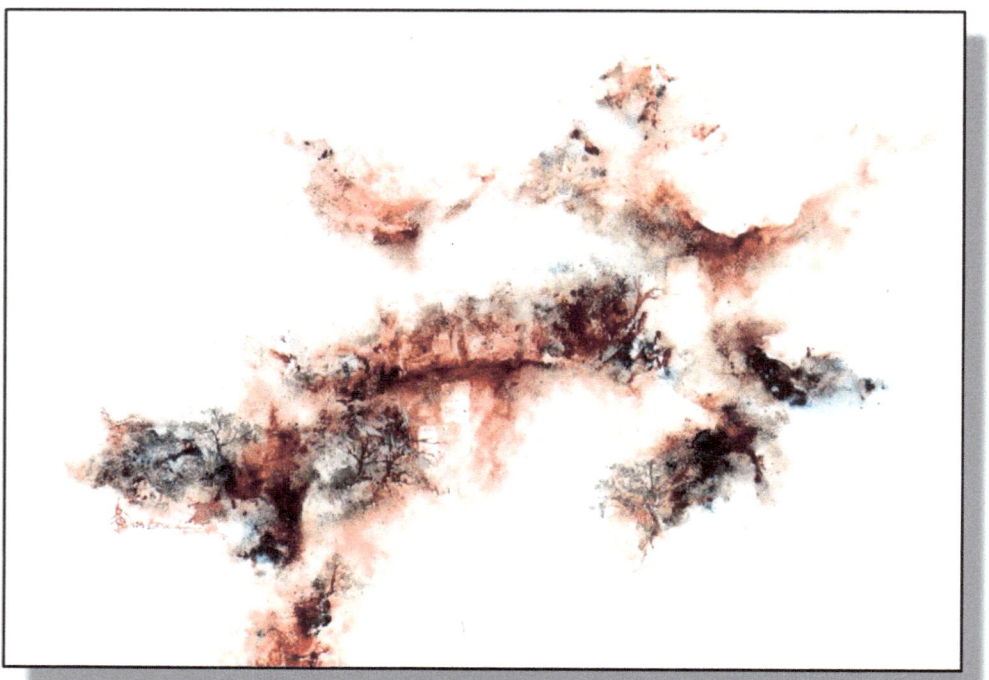

57141 Overhang

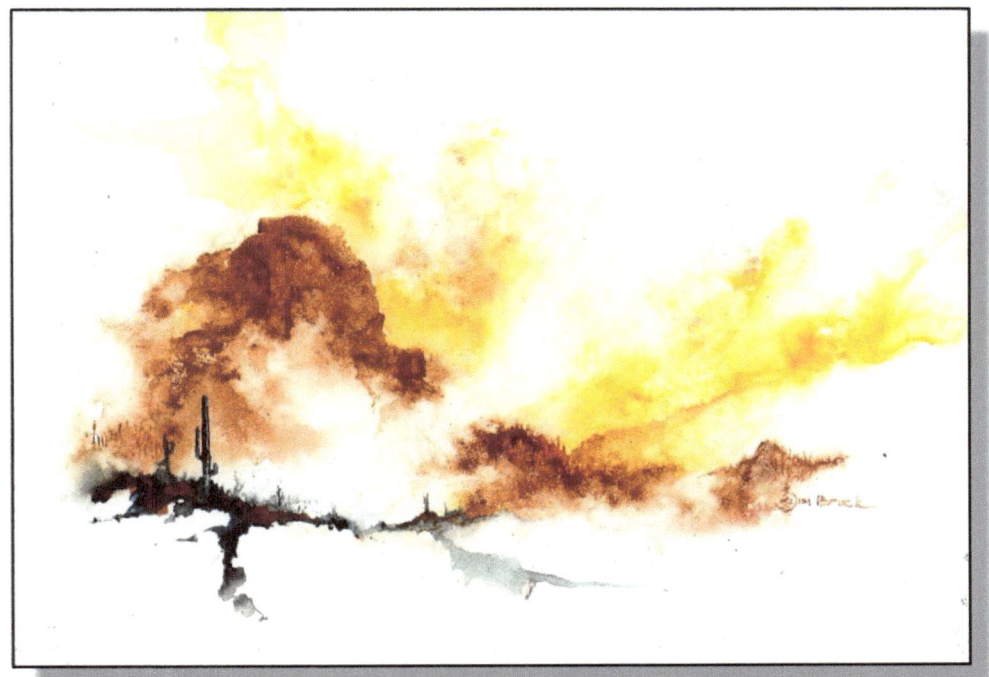

57142 Desert Sunrise

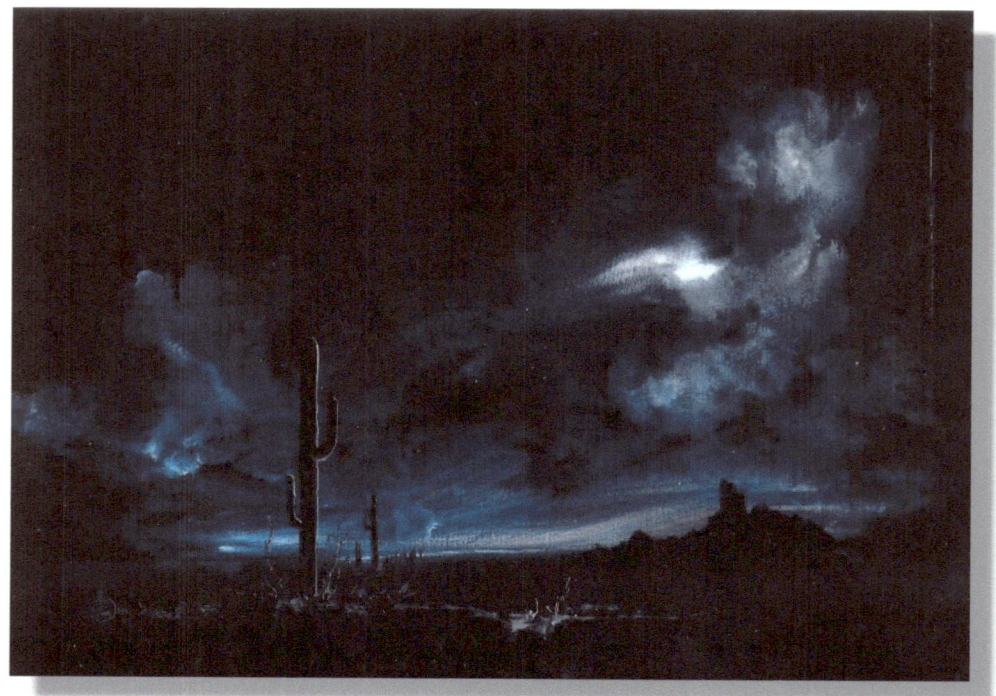

57143 Tucson Evening

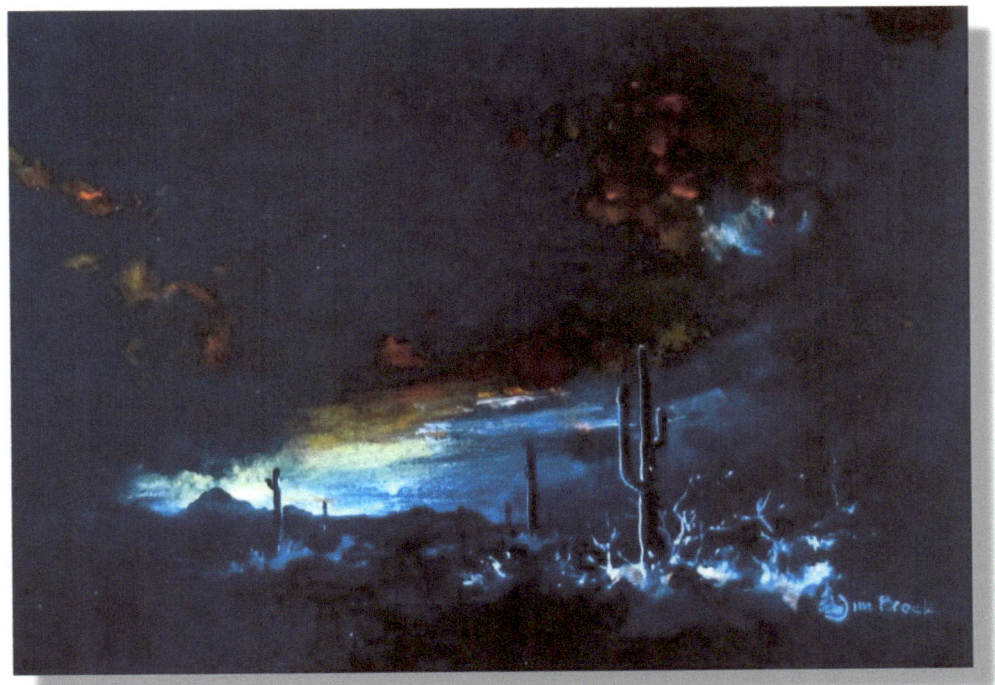

57144 Tucson Sunset

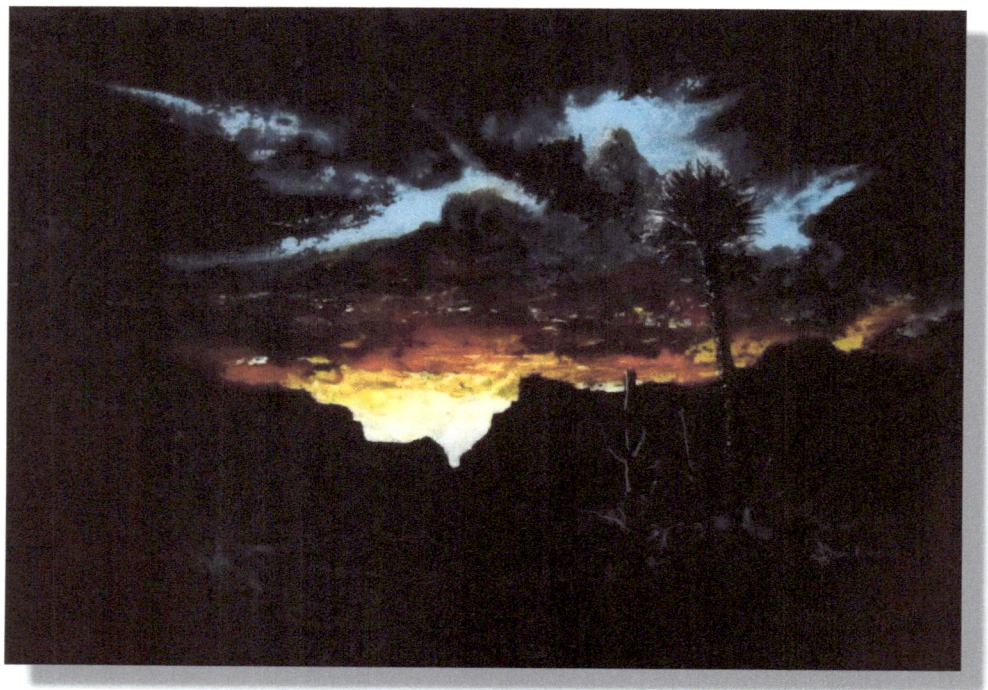

57145 Tucson Sunrise

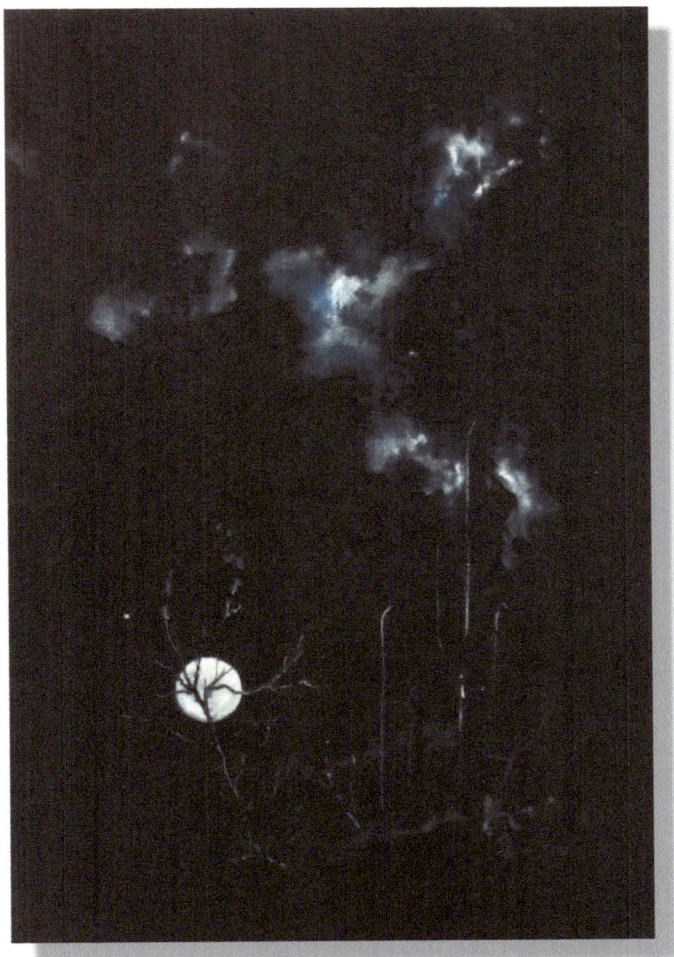

57146 Tucson Moon Rise

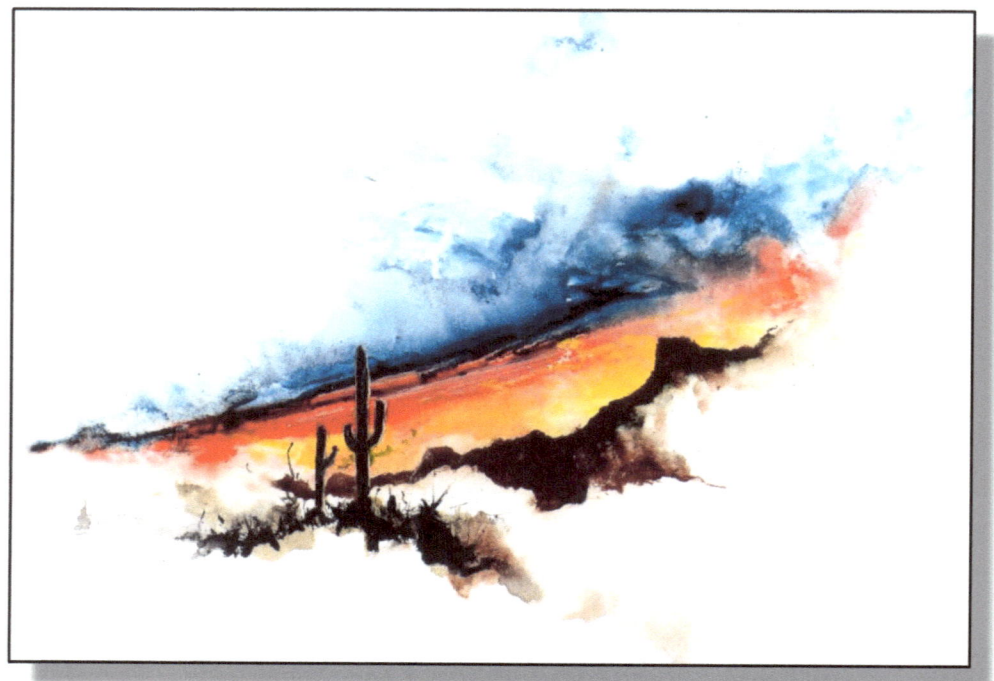

57147 Sunset

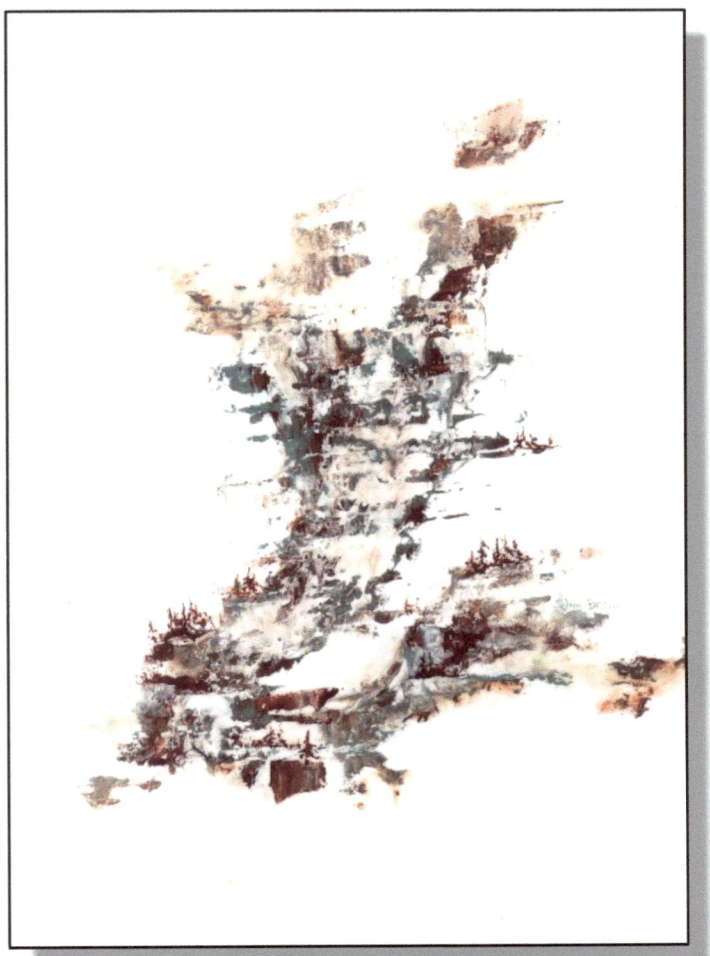

57148 Steps

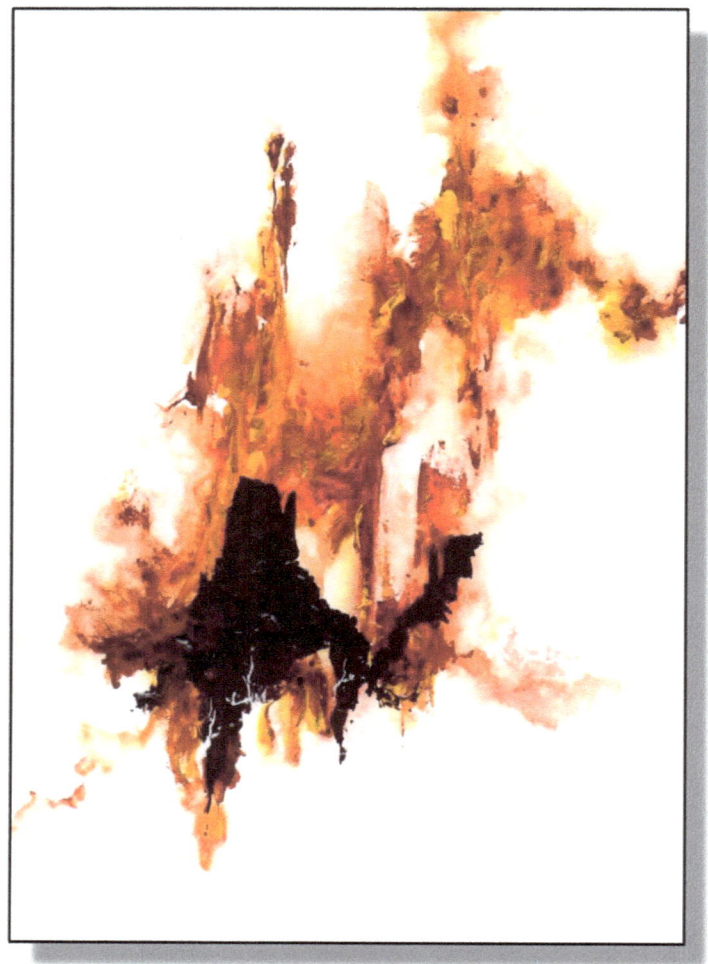

57149 What Will Be

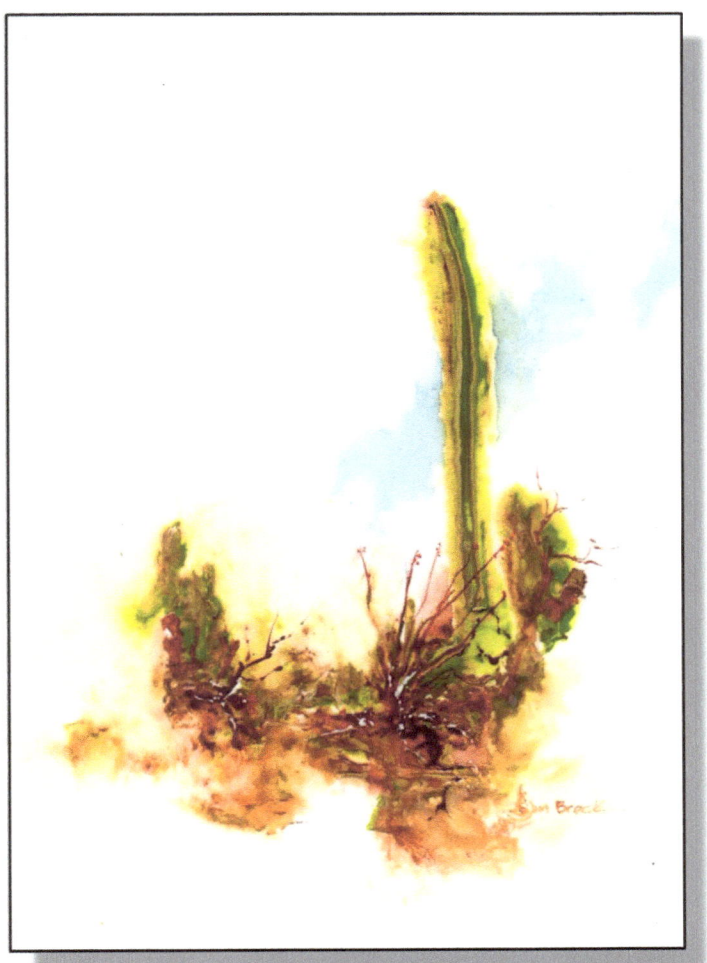

57150 Cactus

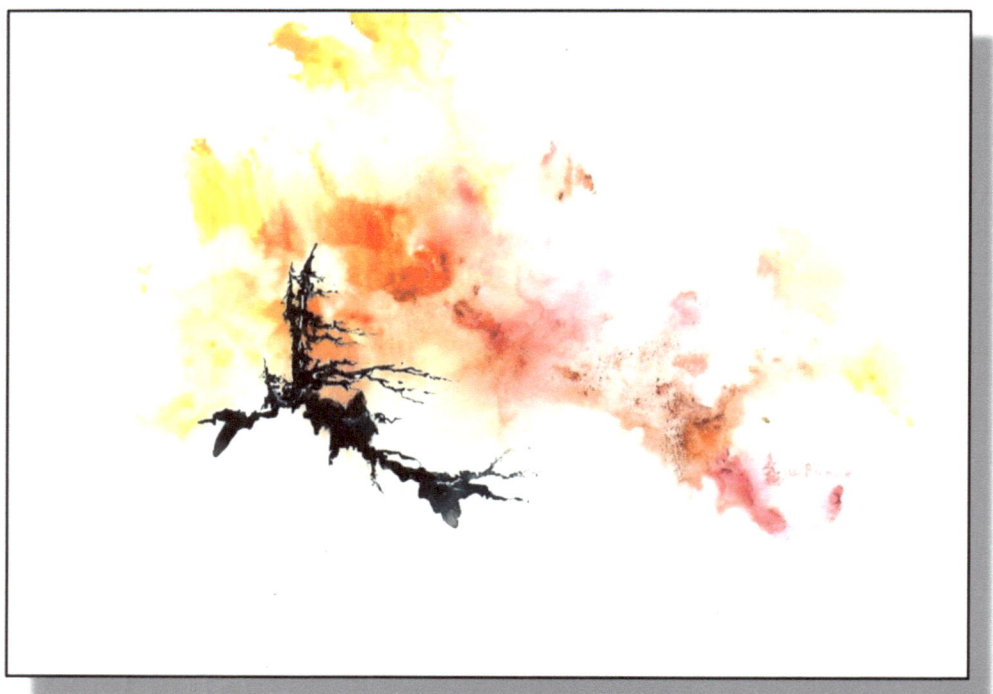

57151 Red Wind

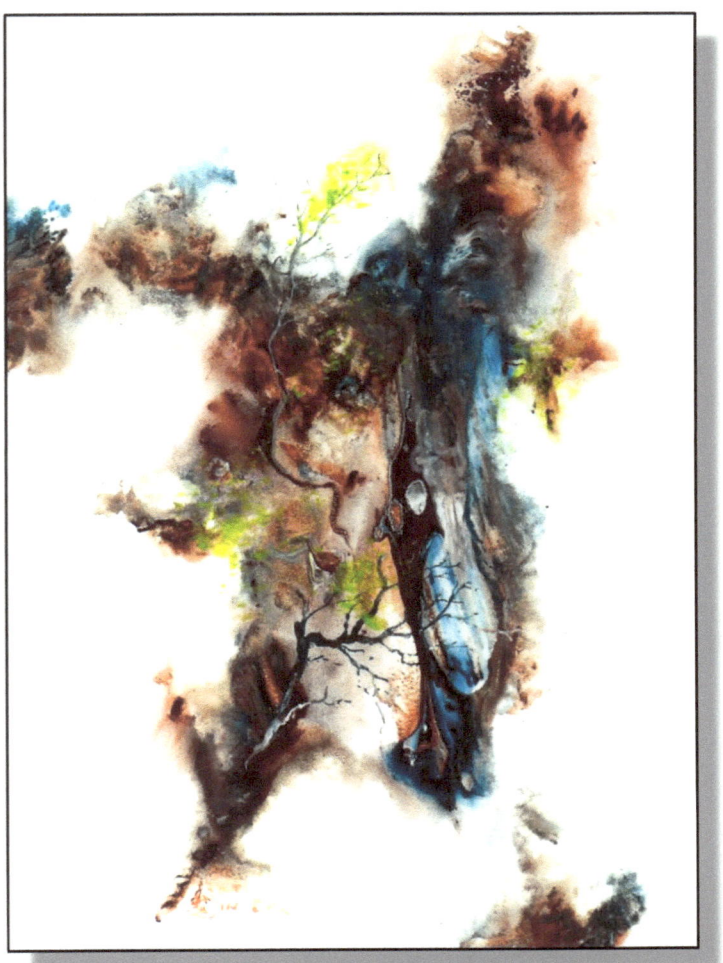

57152 Behind

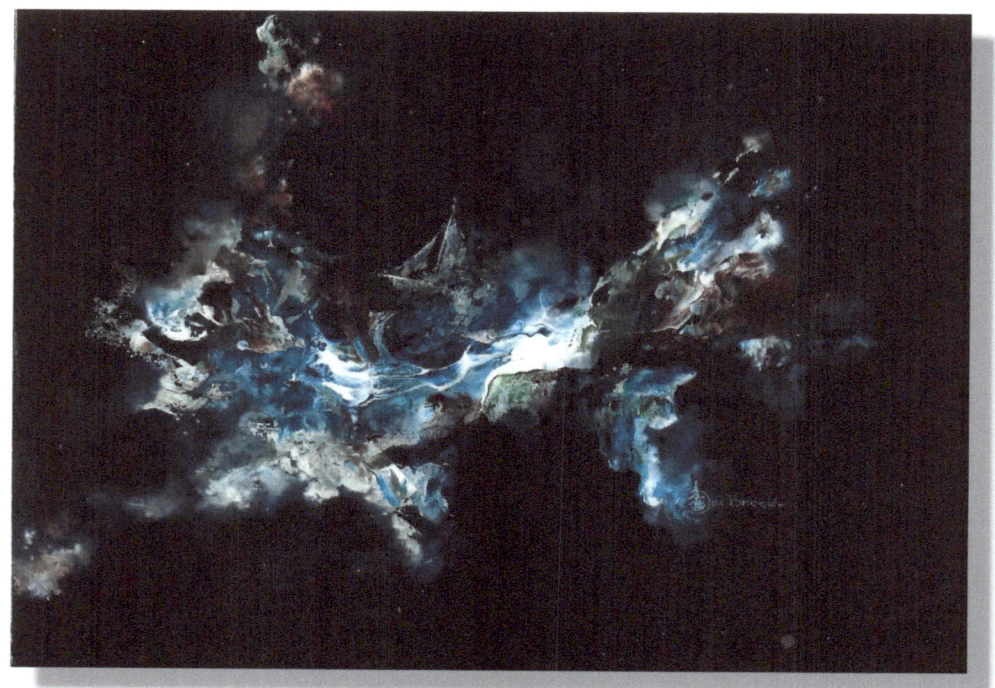

57153 Wave

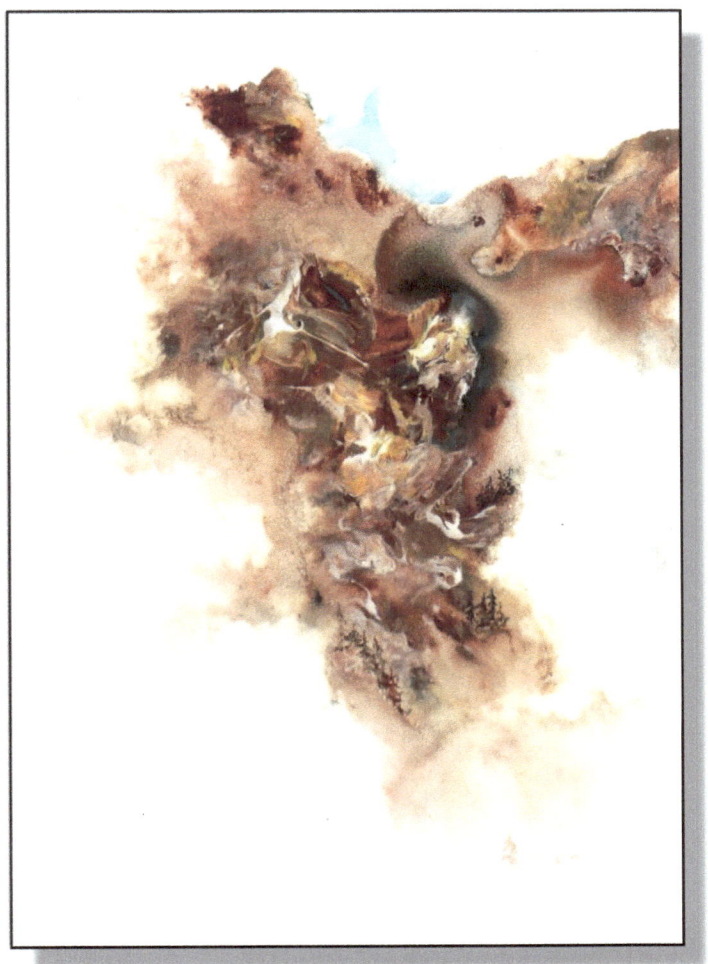

57154 Mountain Core

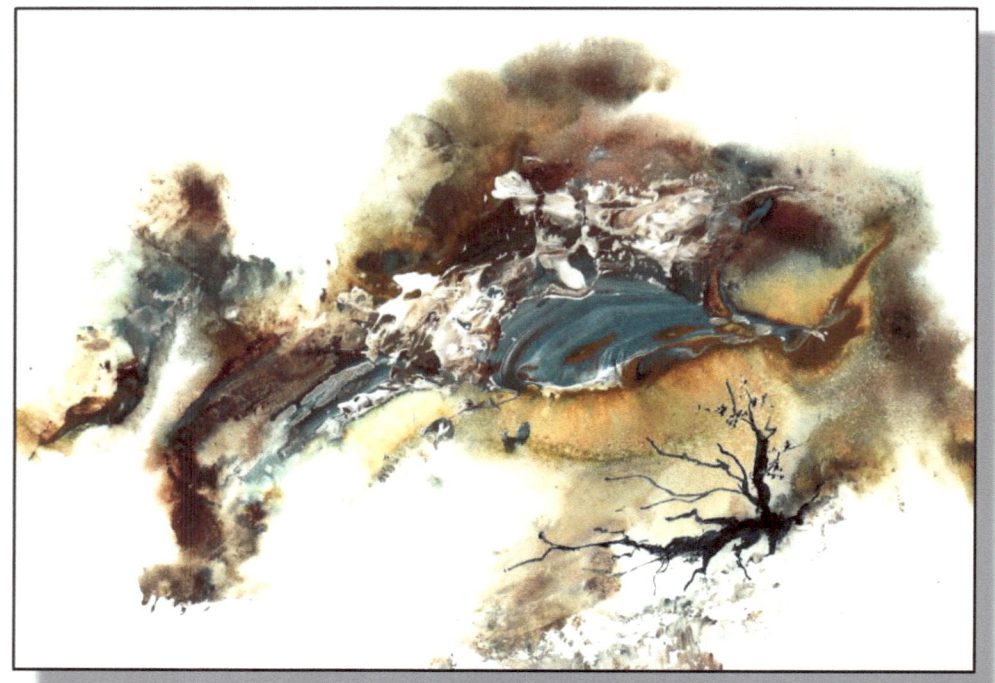

57155 Tsu

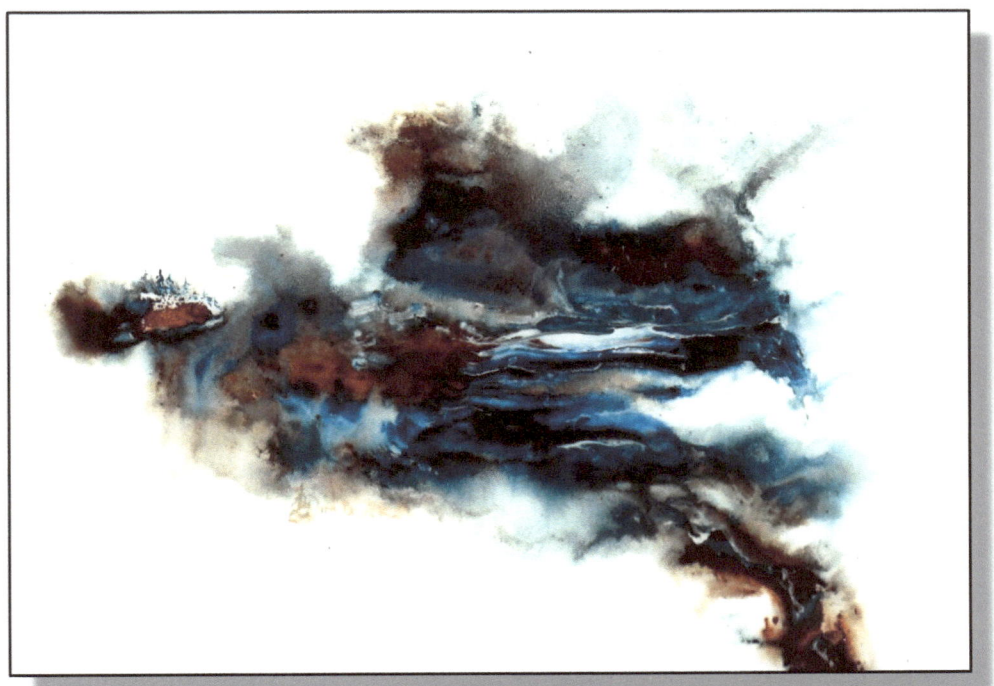

57156 Top of the Falls

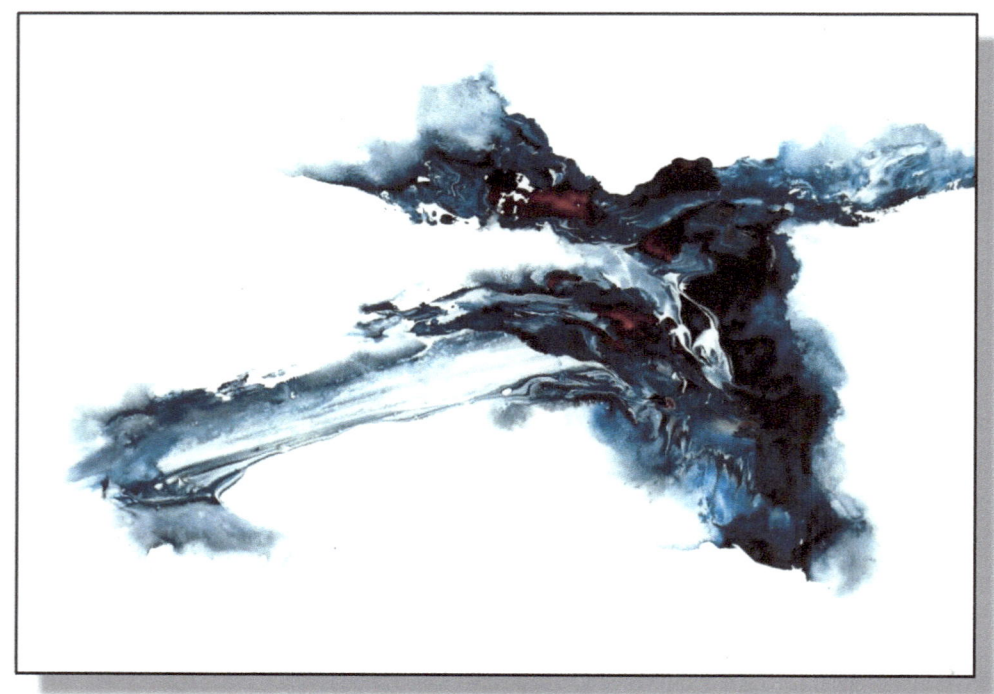

57157 Bleeding Glacier

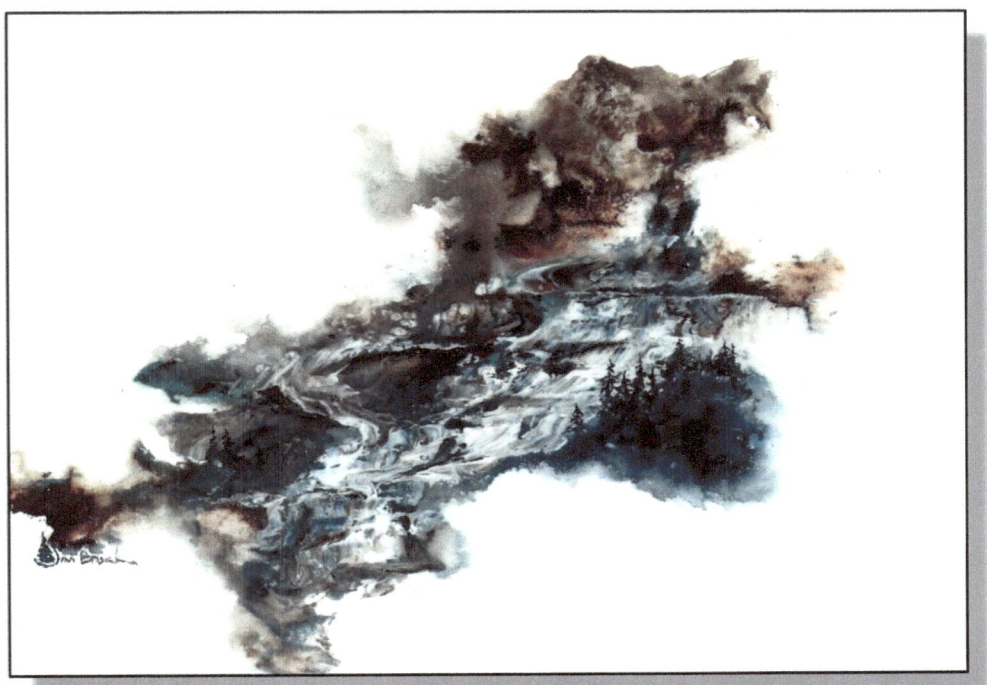

57158 Falls Crossing

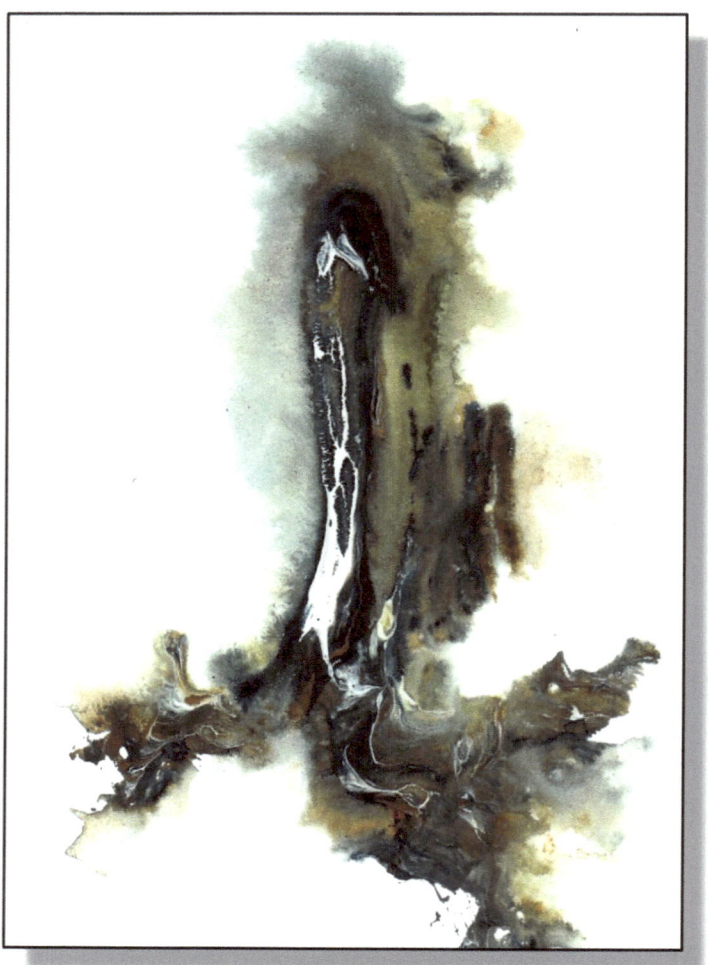

57159 Grotto Springs

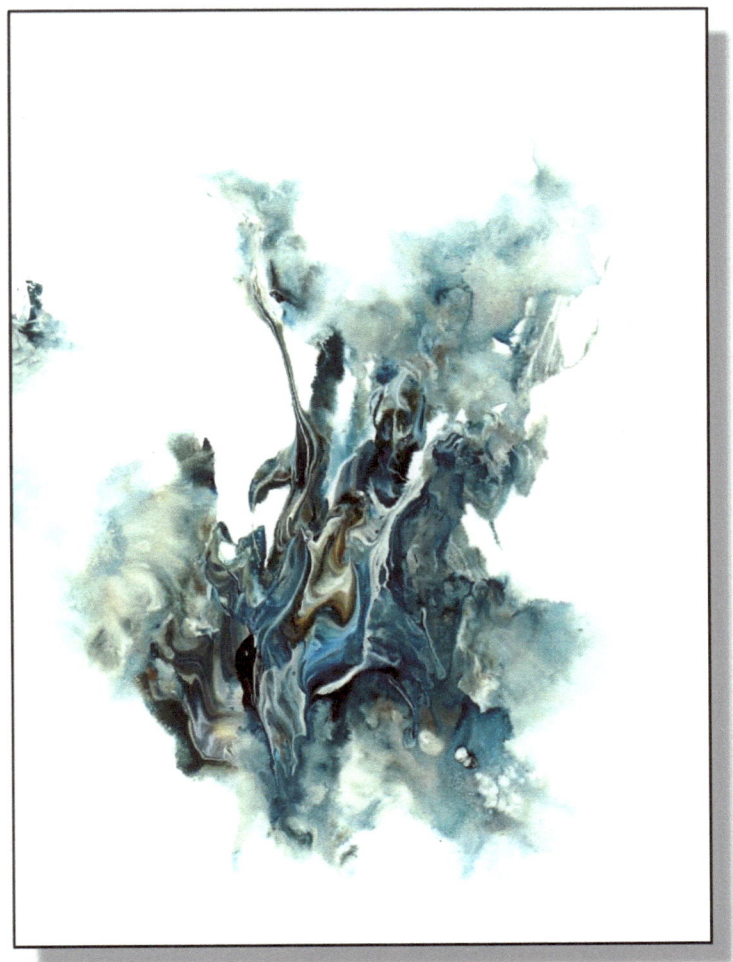

57160 Dryad What Have We Done?

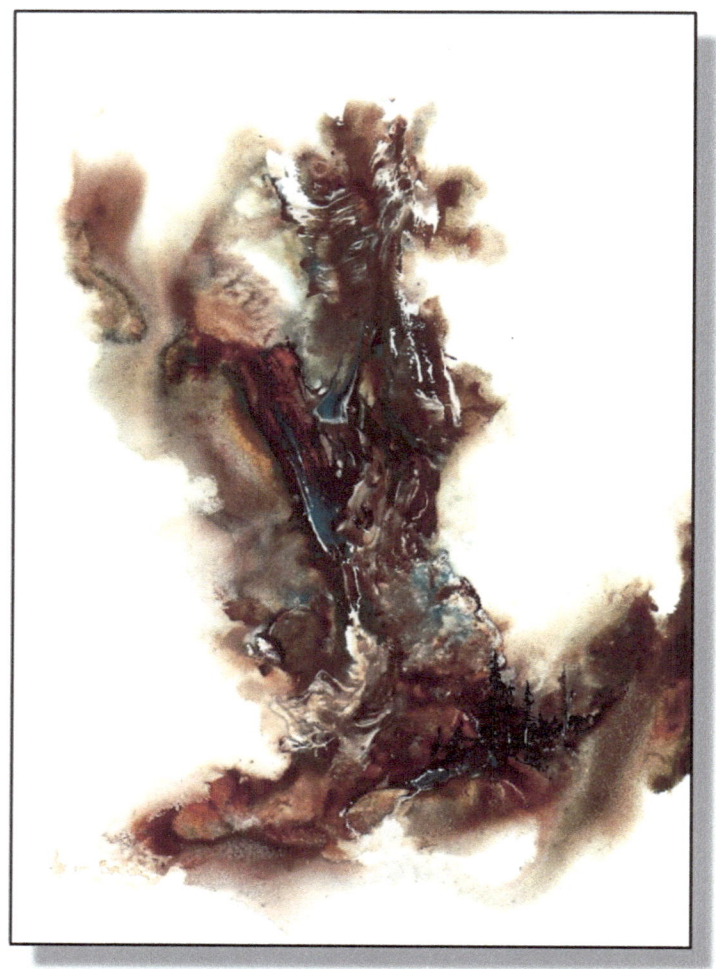

57161 Slide

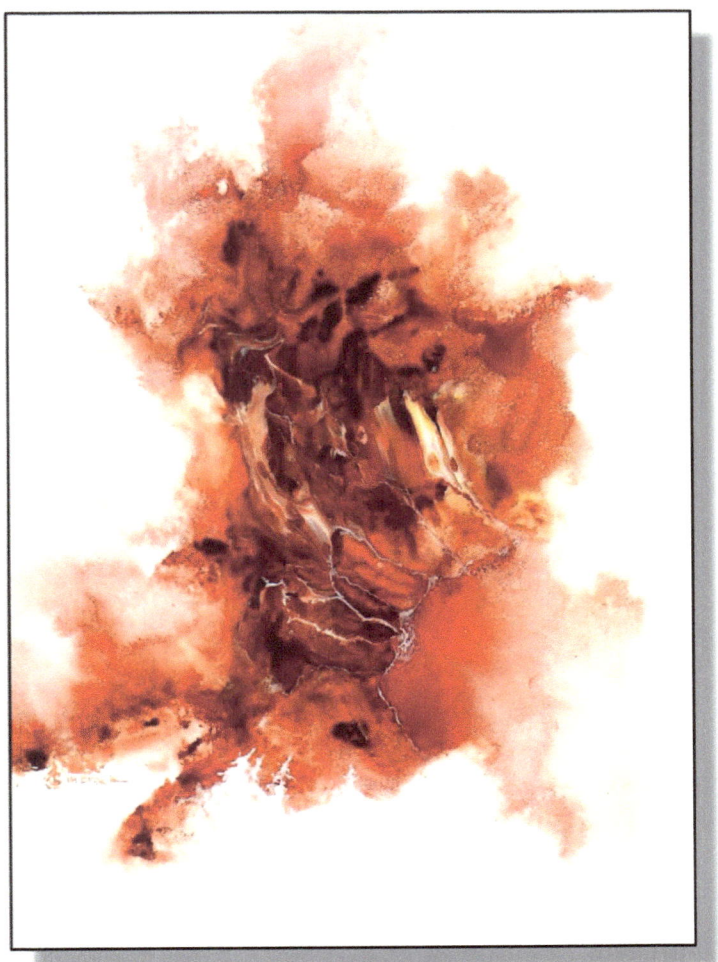

57162 Feed the Pool

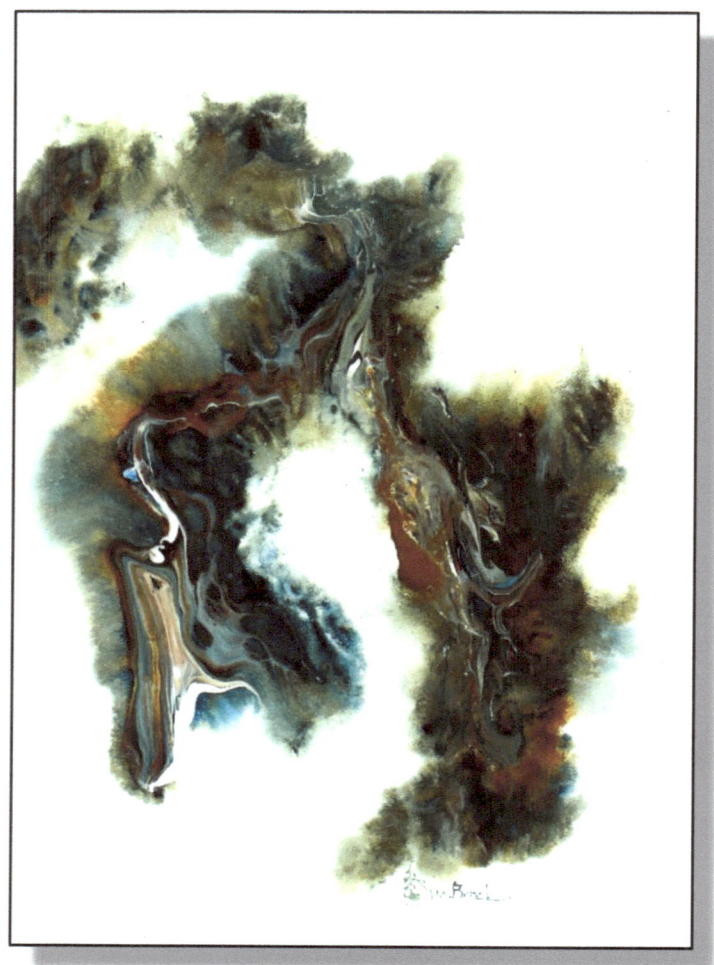

57163 Roots

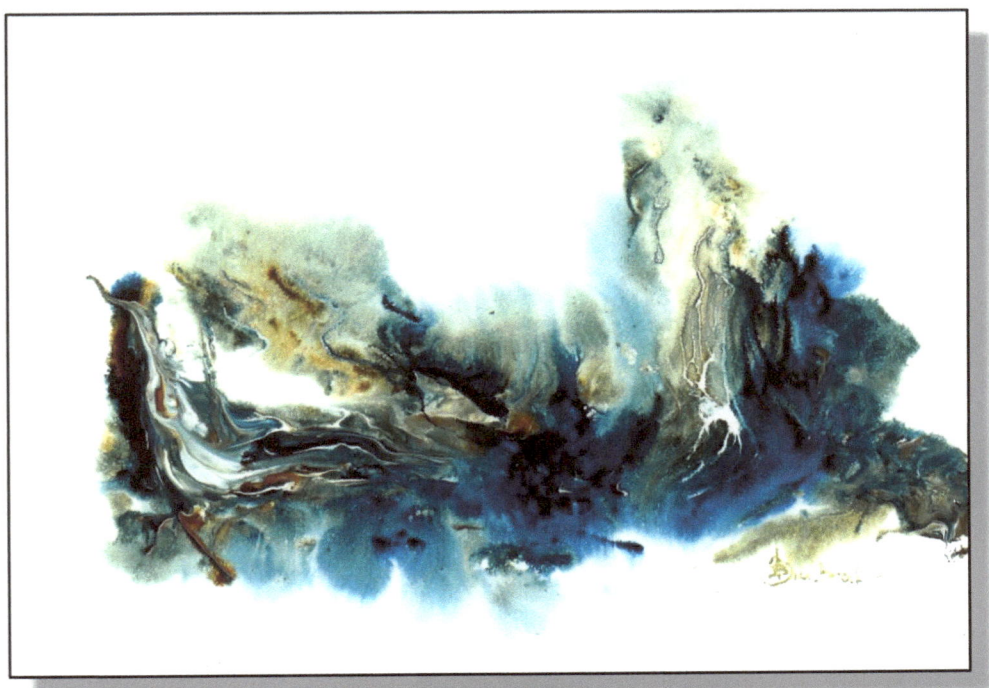

57164 Gene Pool

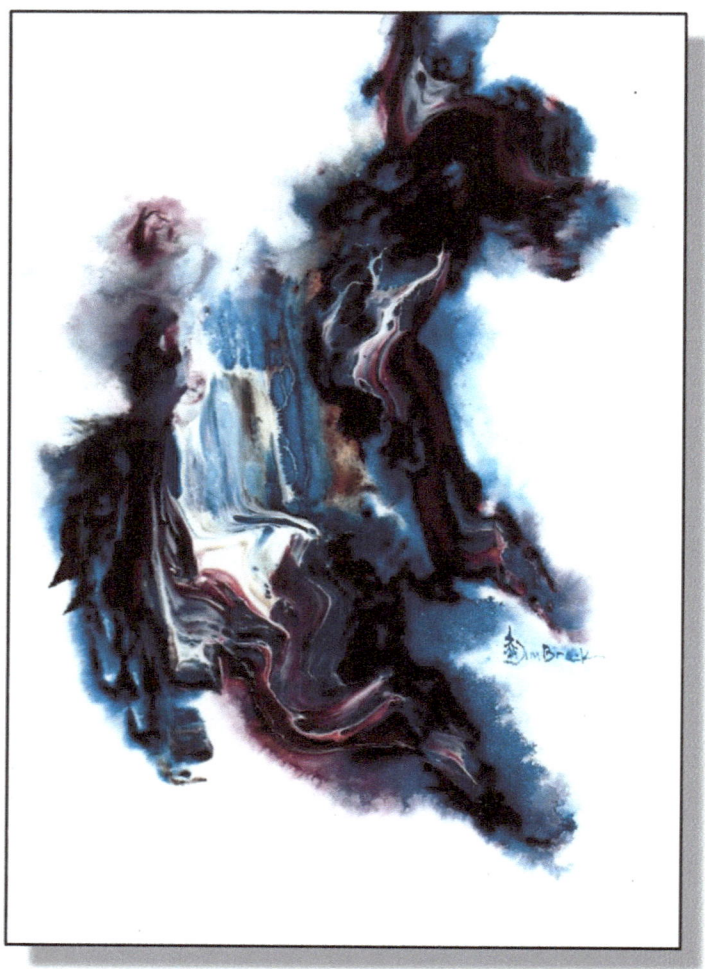

57165 Rainbow Falls

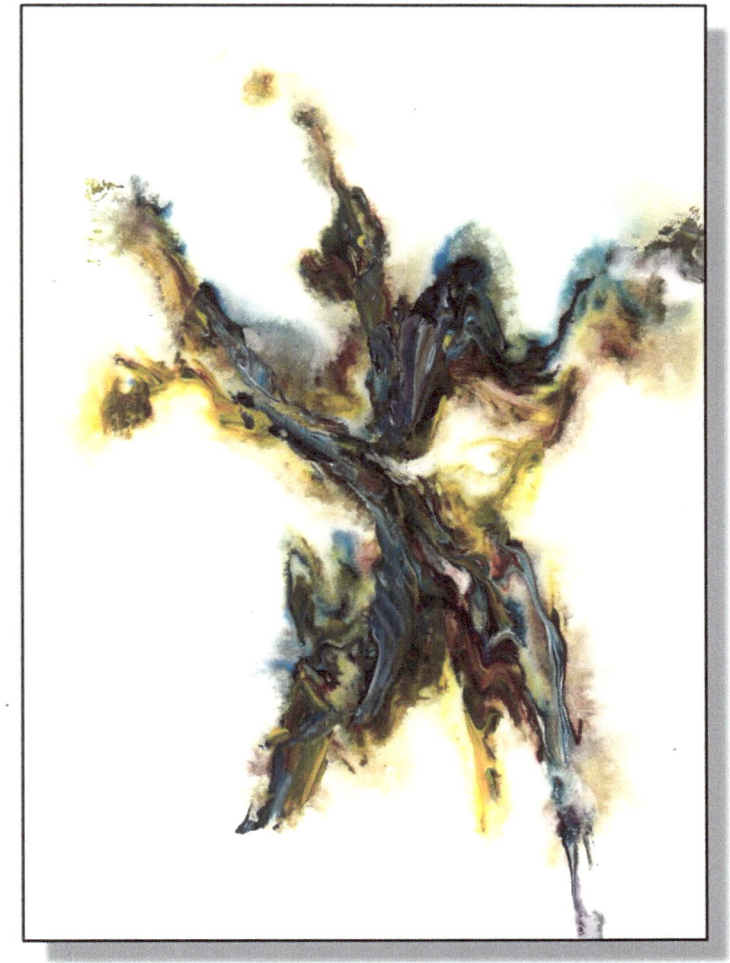

57166 Sweet Spot

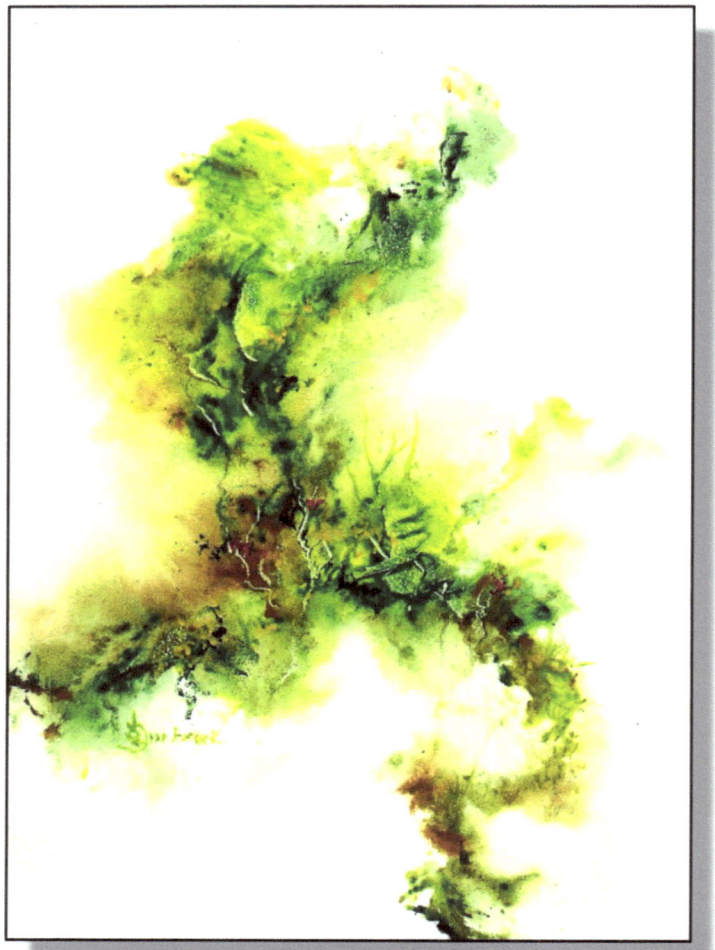

57167 Spring-ing

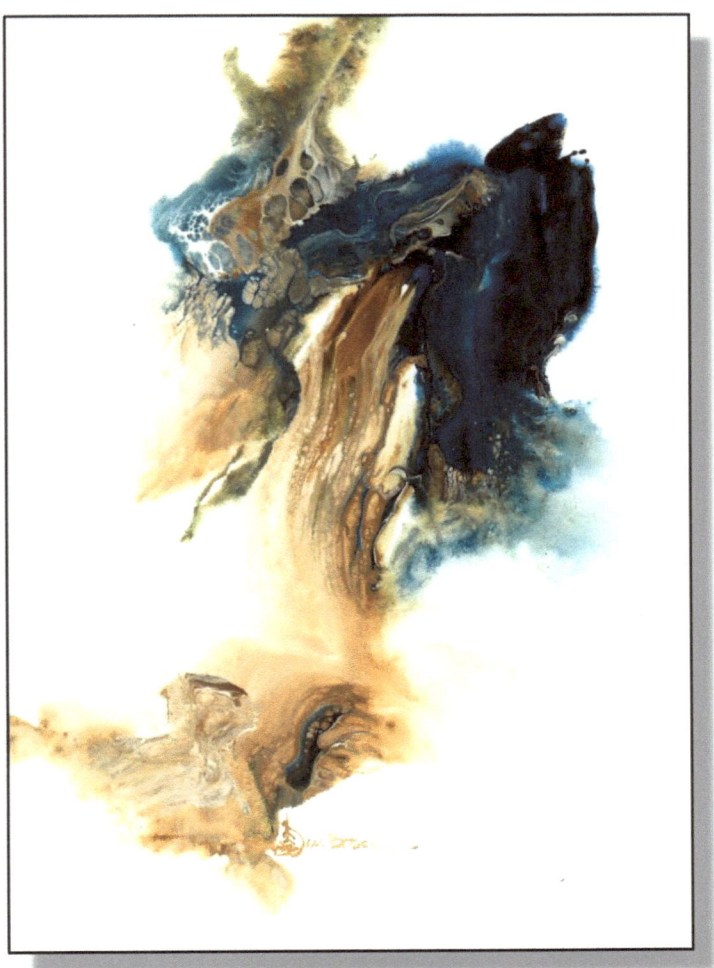

57168 Mixing Agate

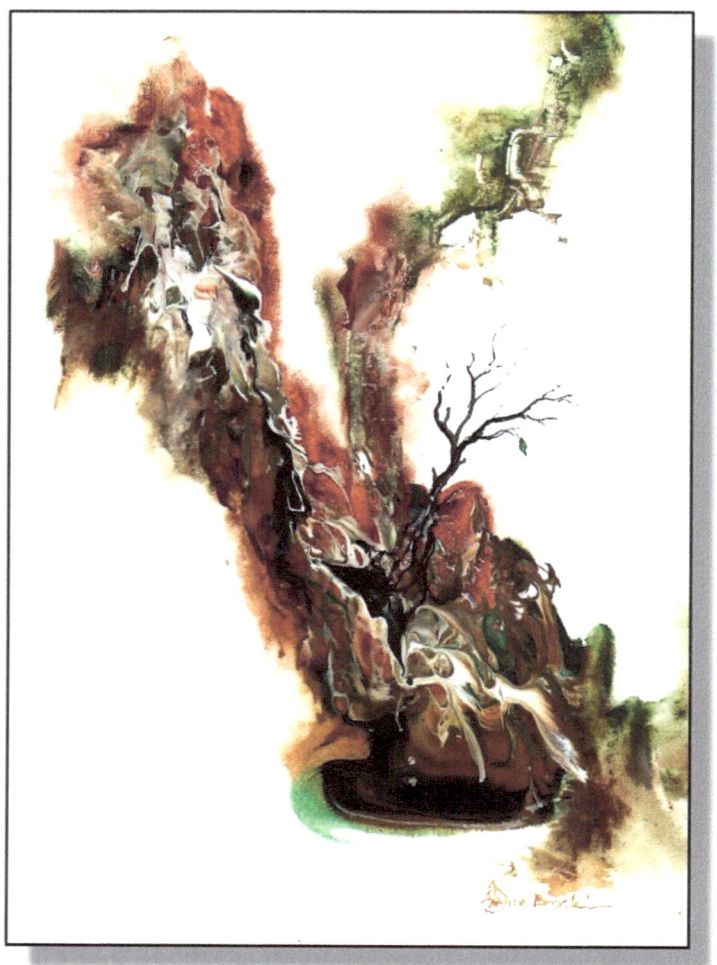

57169 How Now Chlorophyll

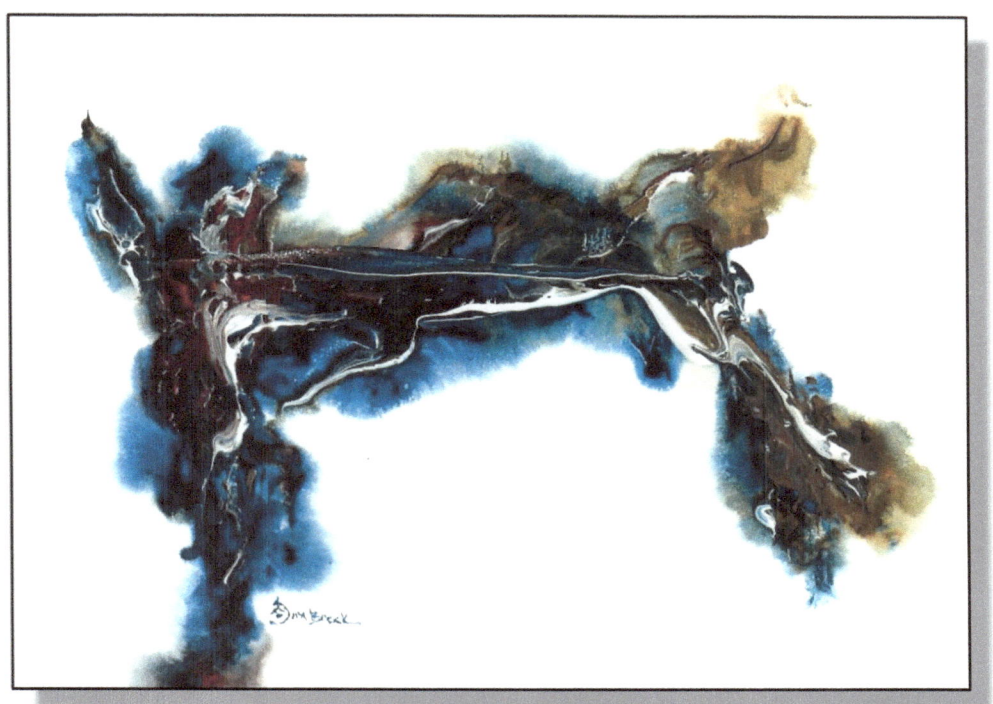

57170 Below Pond Level

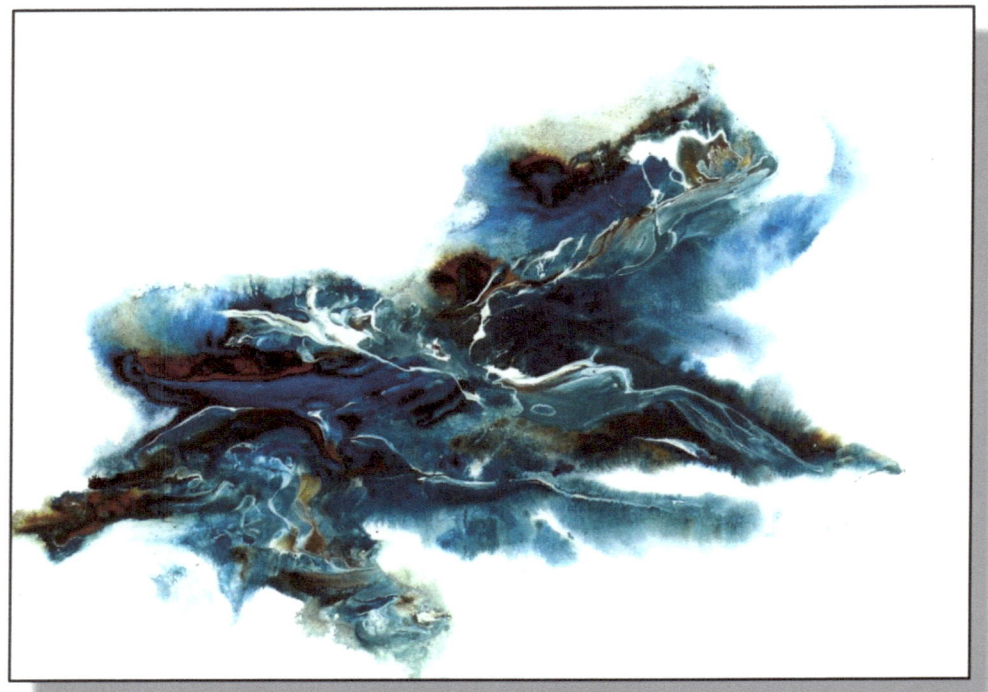

57171 Surf's Up

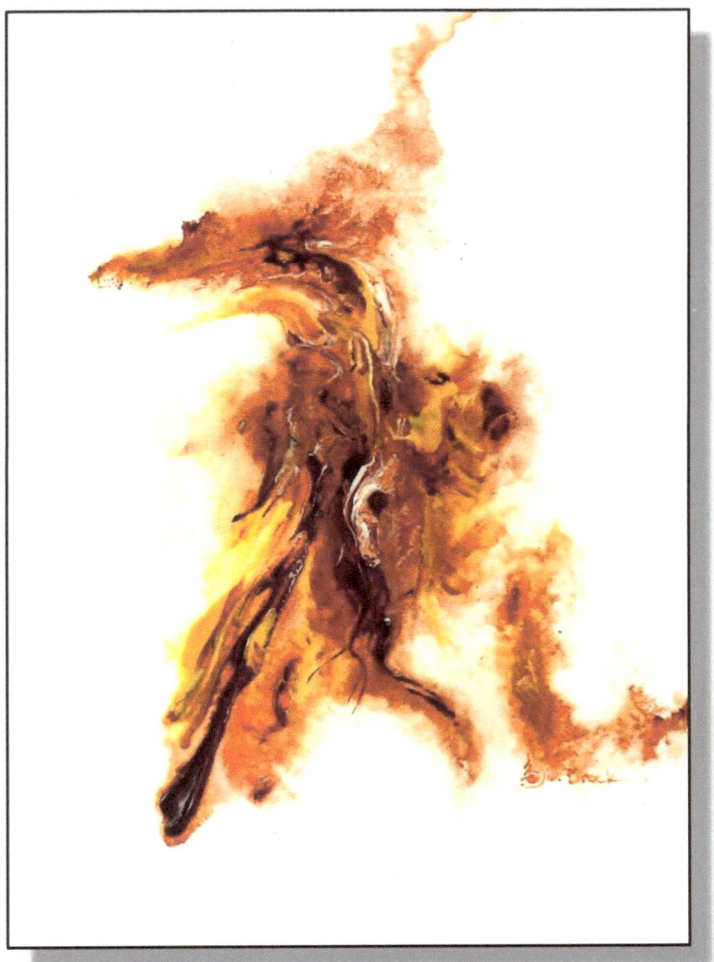

57172 Fumie

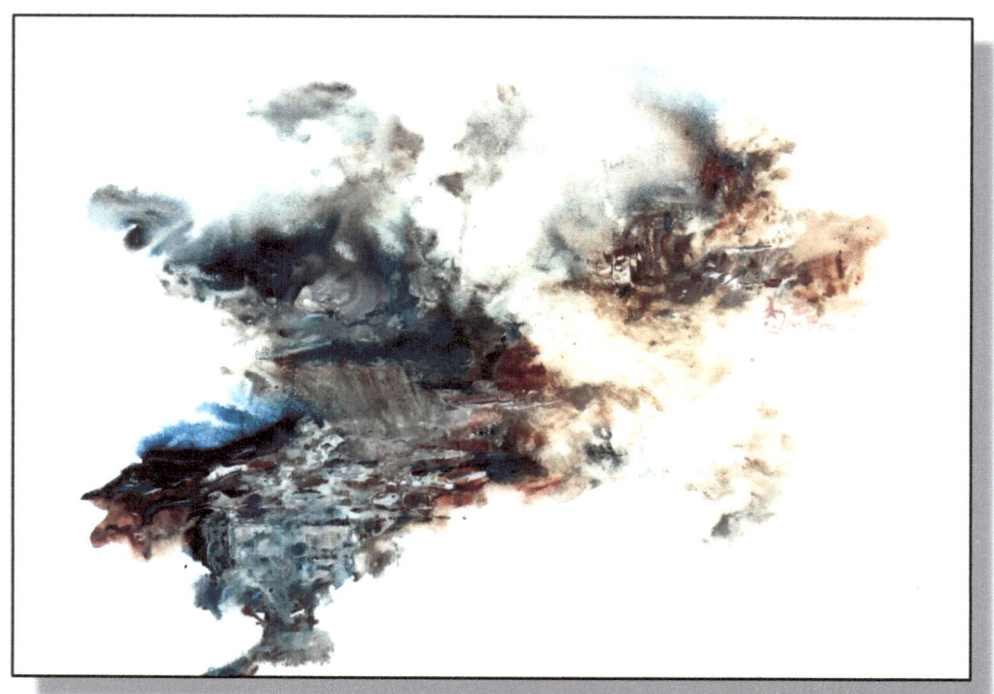

57173 Desert Flood

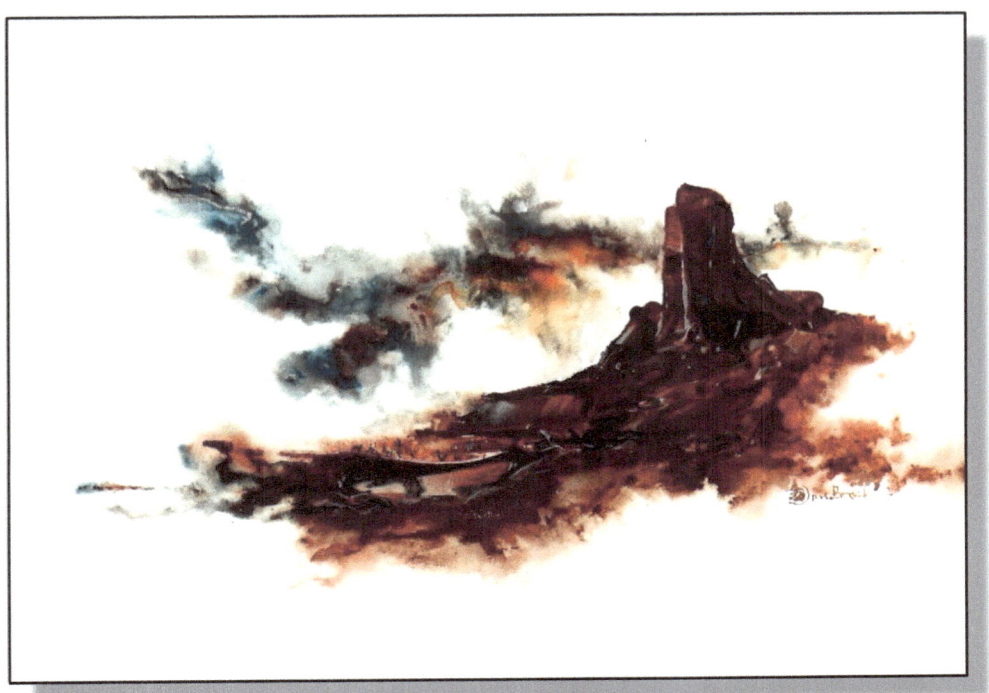

57174 Spire

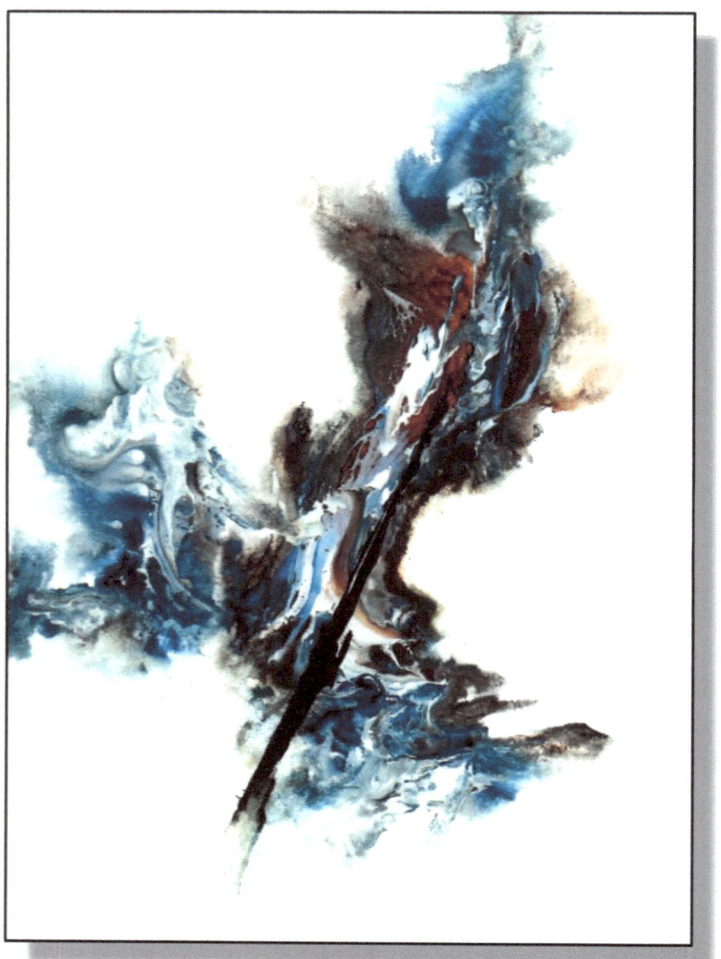

57175 Fracking

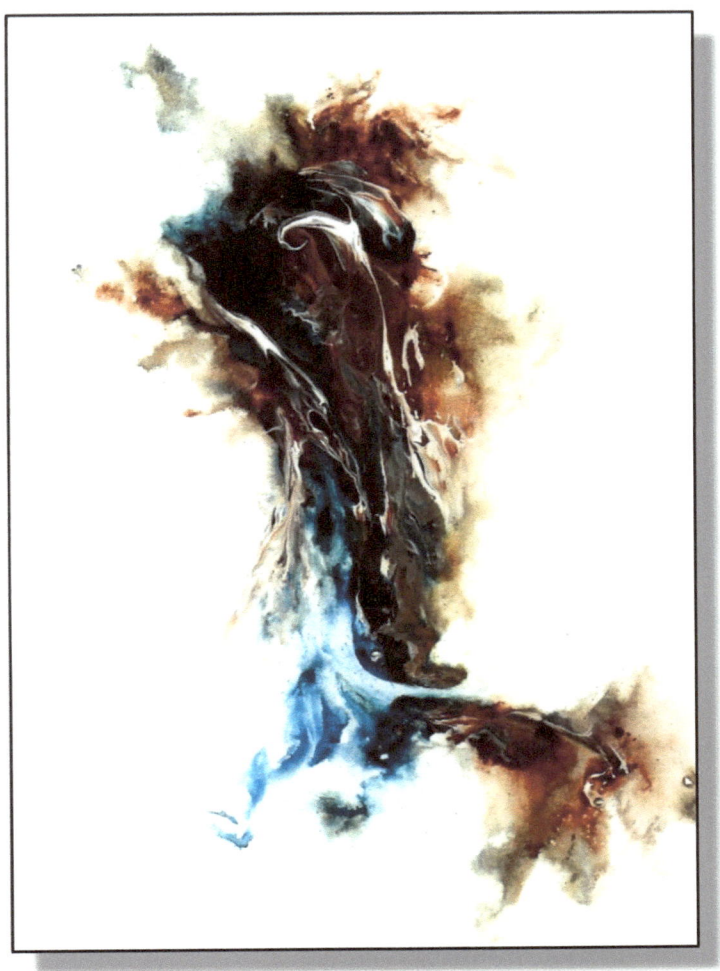

57176 Flow

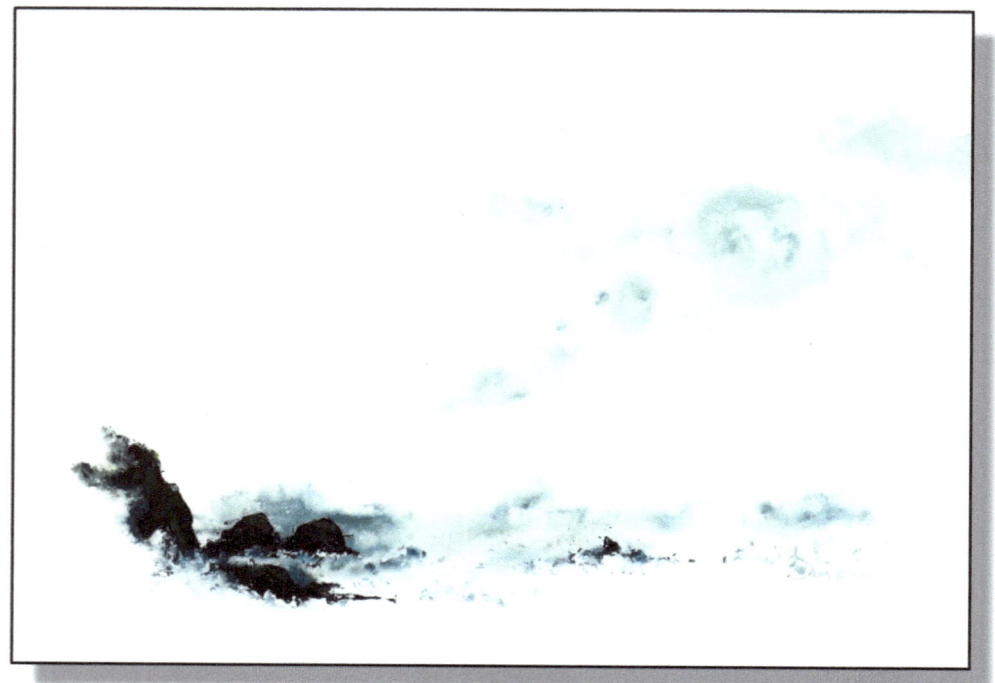

57177 Foggy Coast

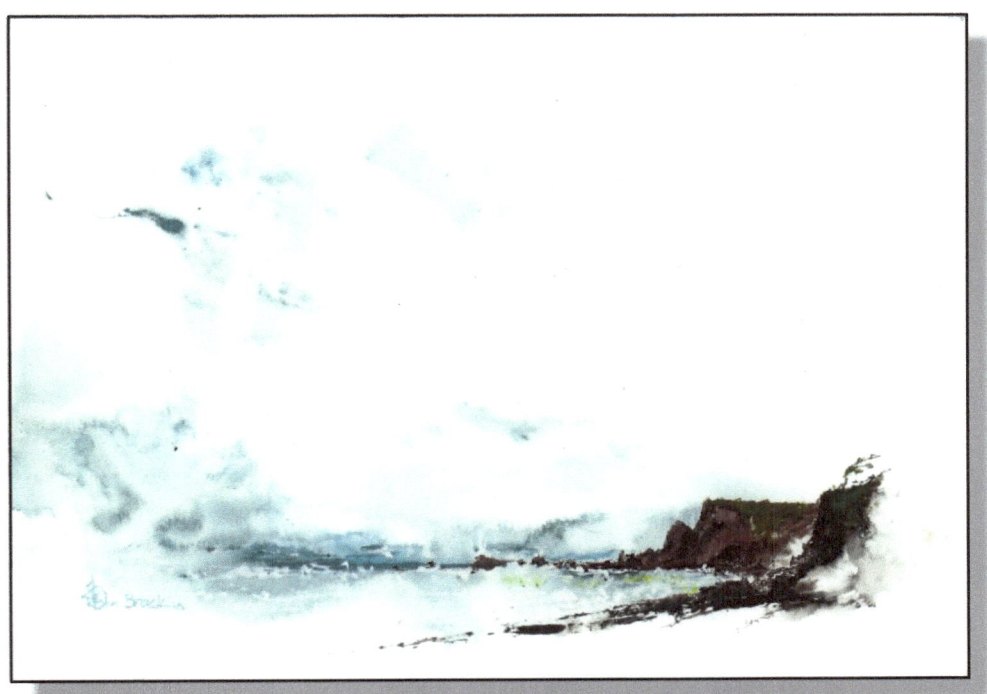

57178 Comes Fog

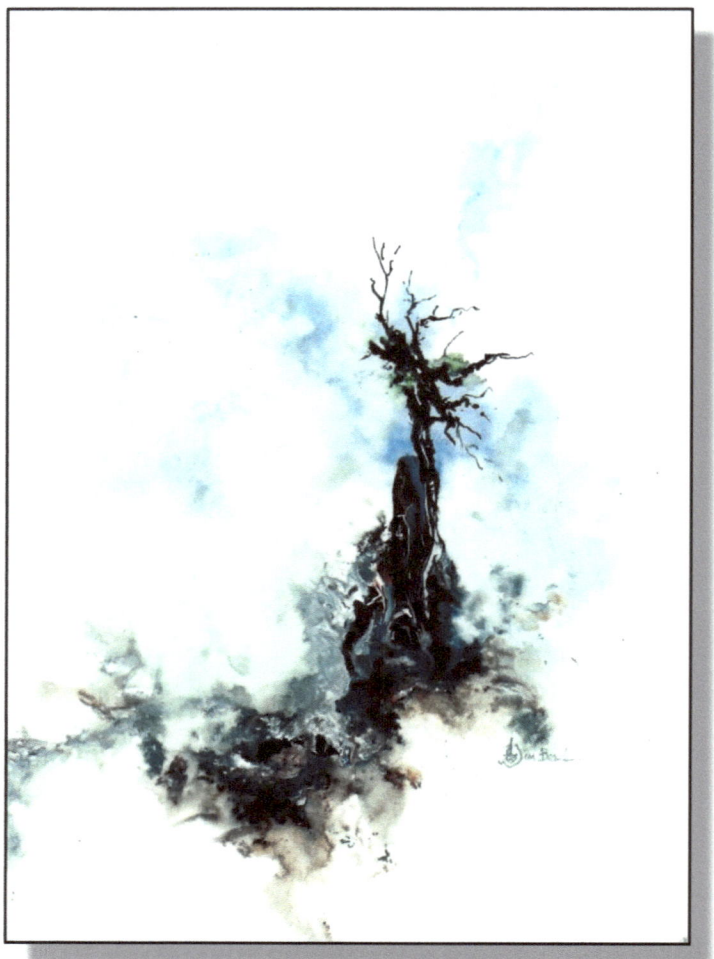

57179 Hanging On

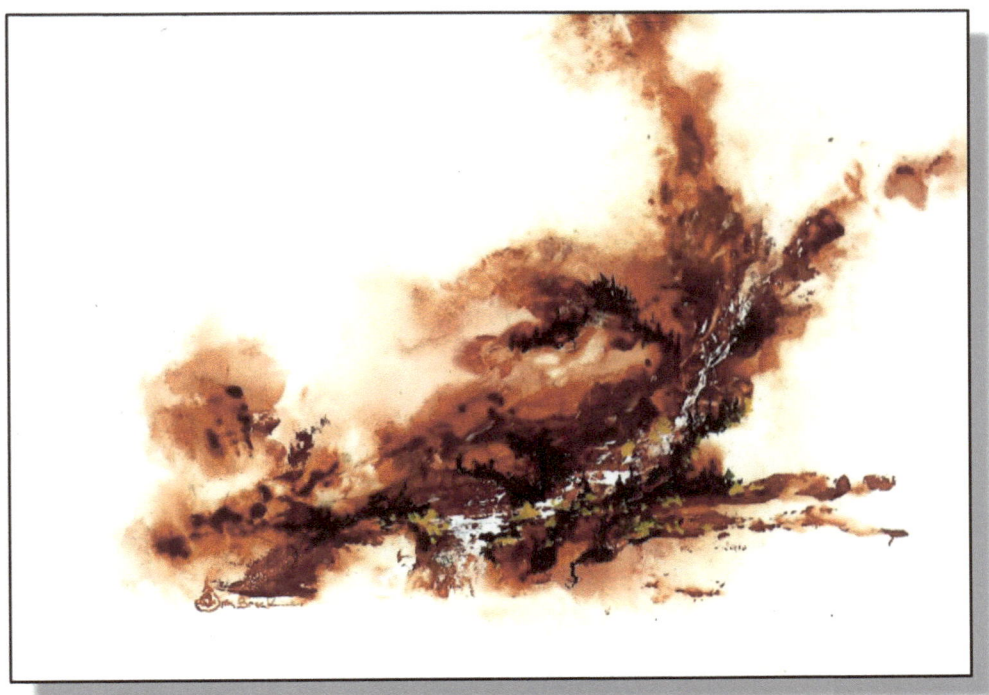

57180 Down Hill

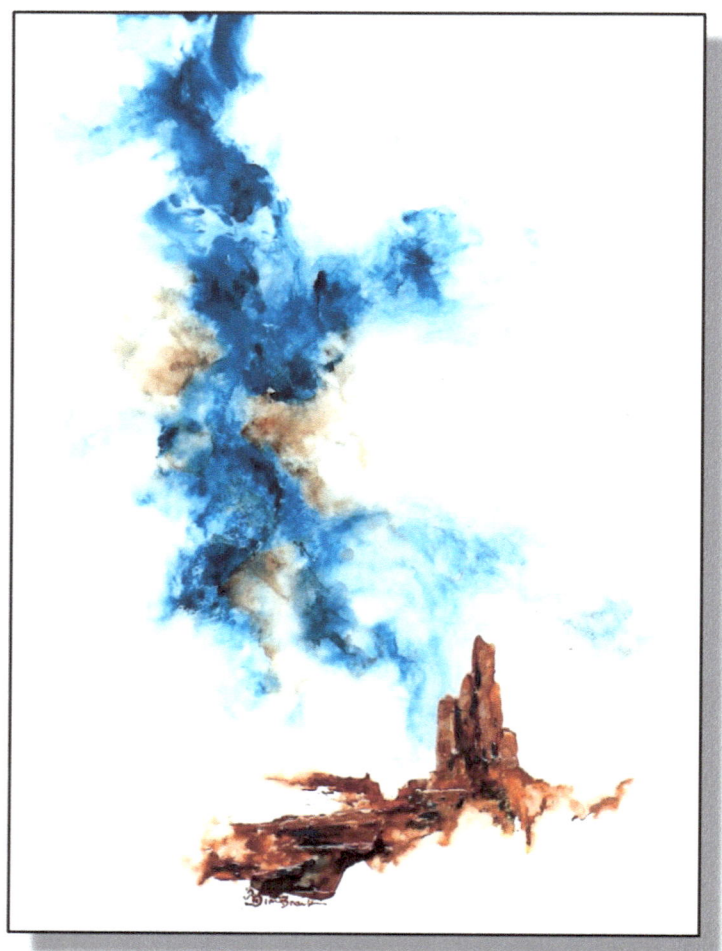

57181 Monument

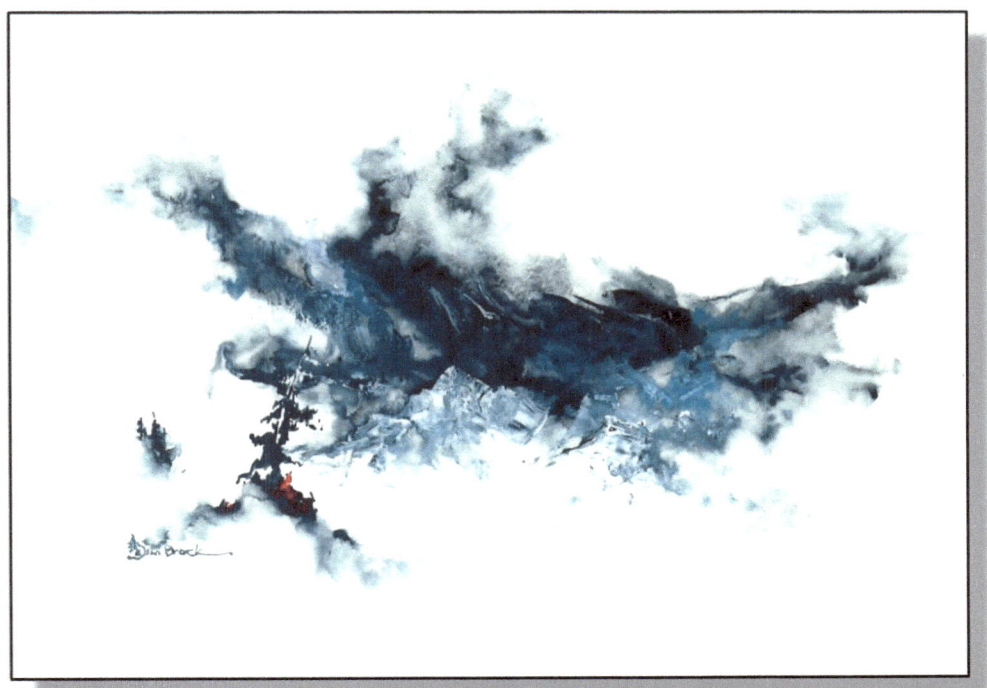

57182 Crest

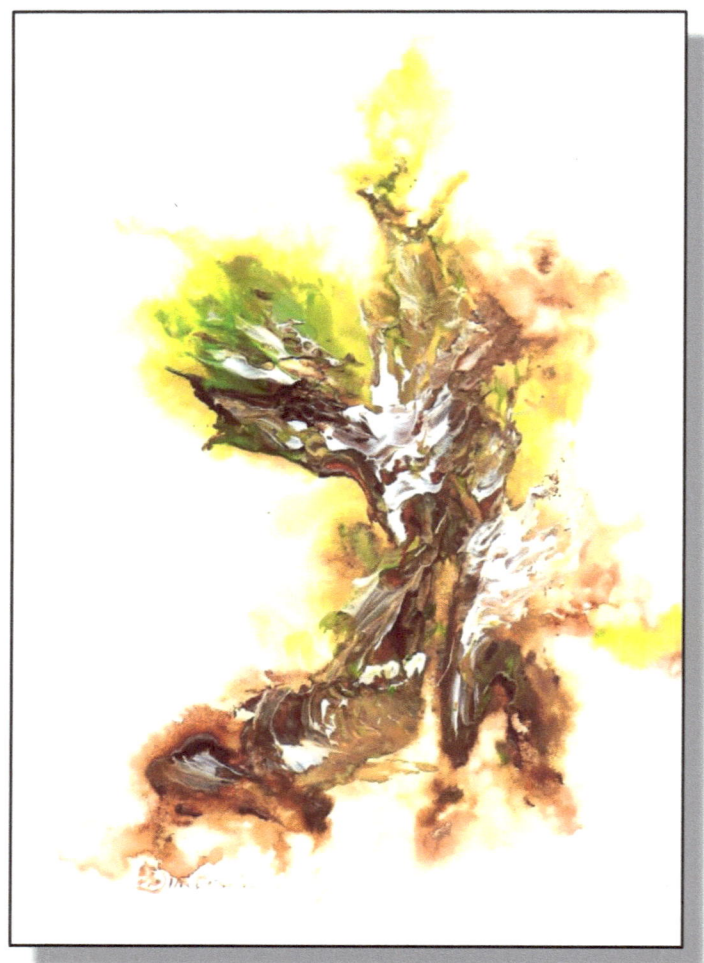

57183 Trunk

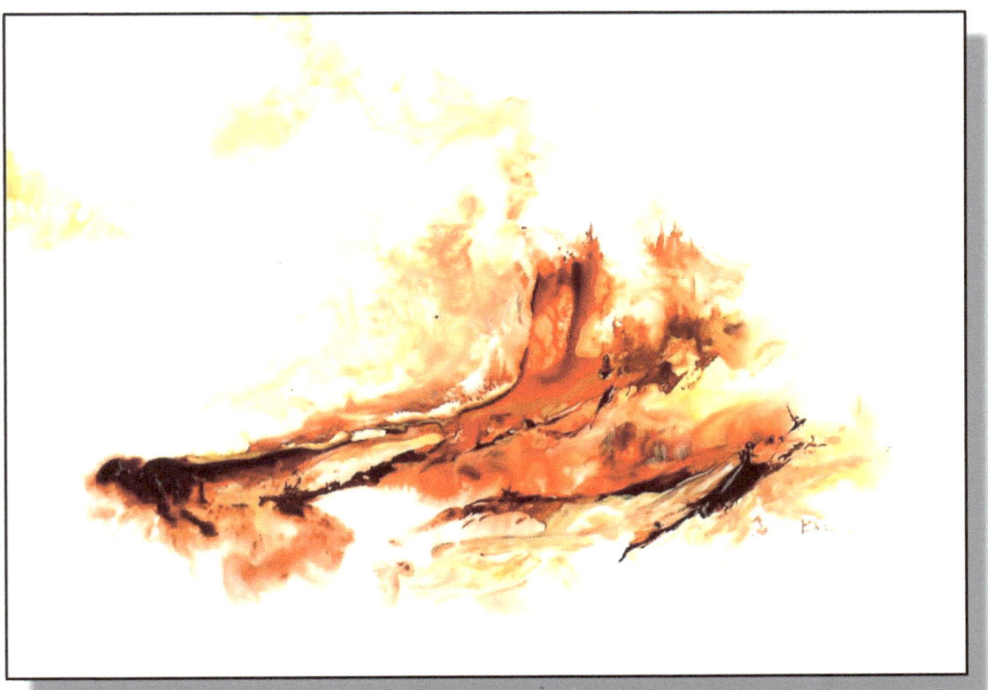

57184 Mountain Core

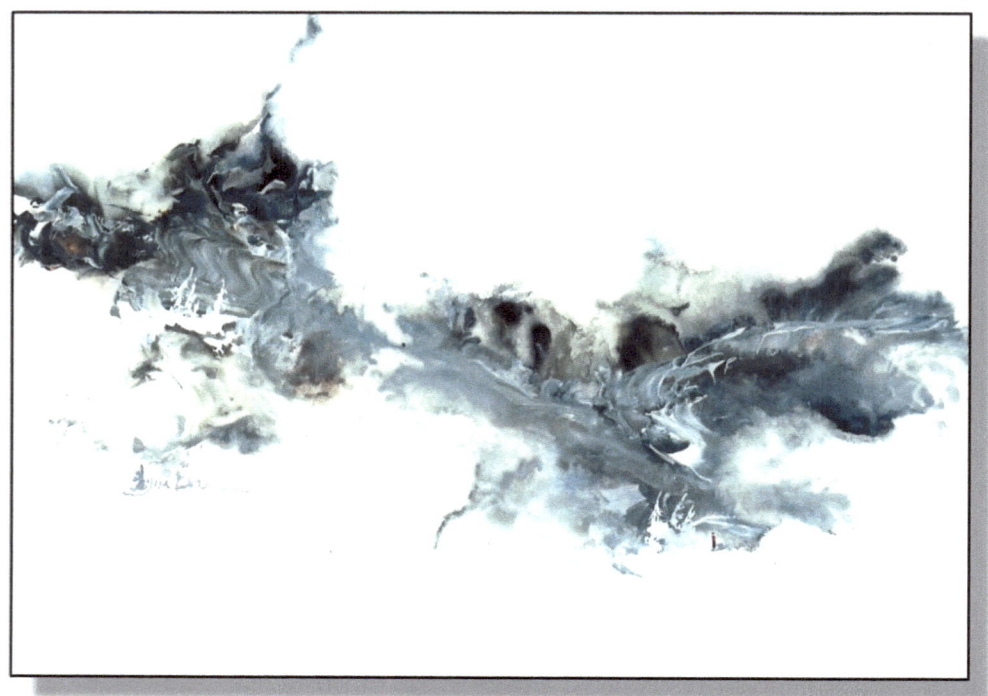

57185 Creek Flow

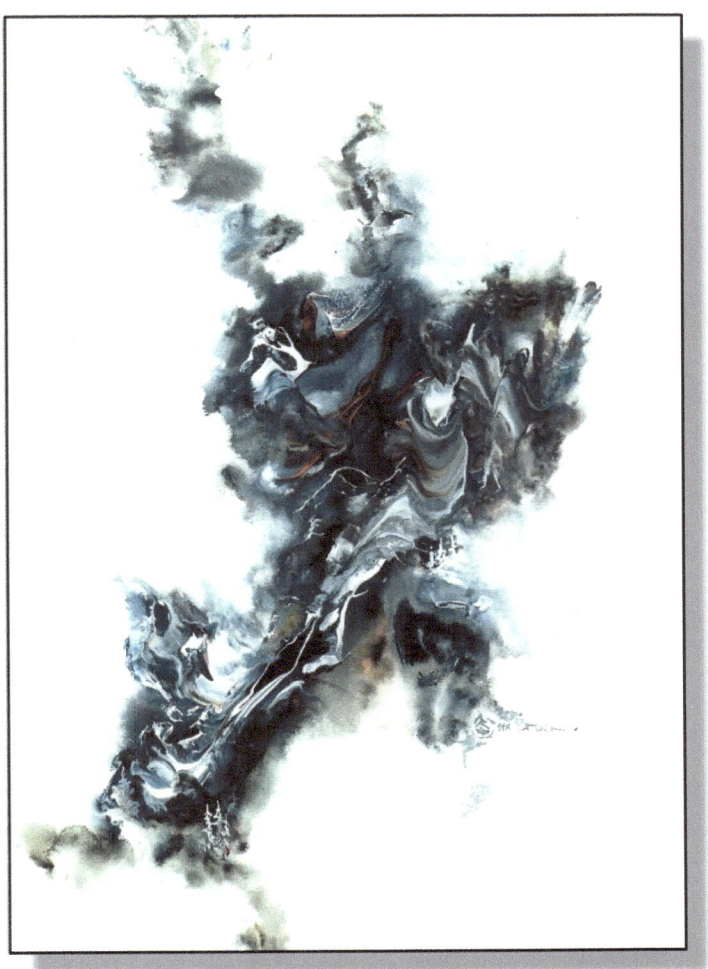

57186 Downhill

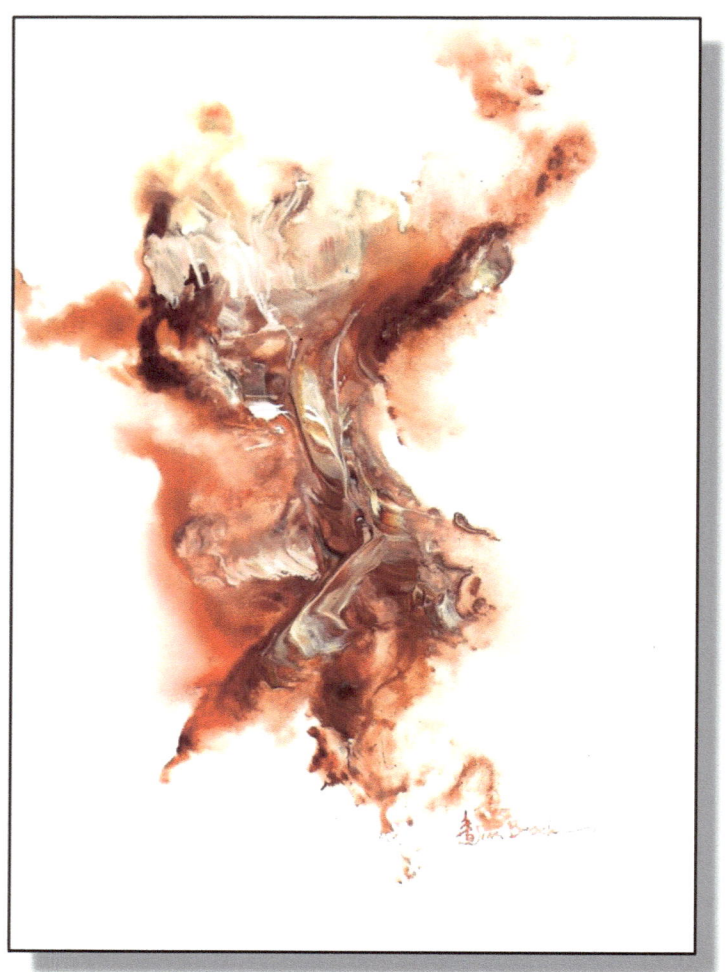

57187 Tree Flow

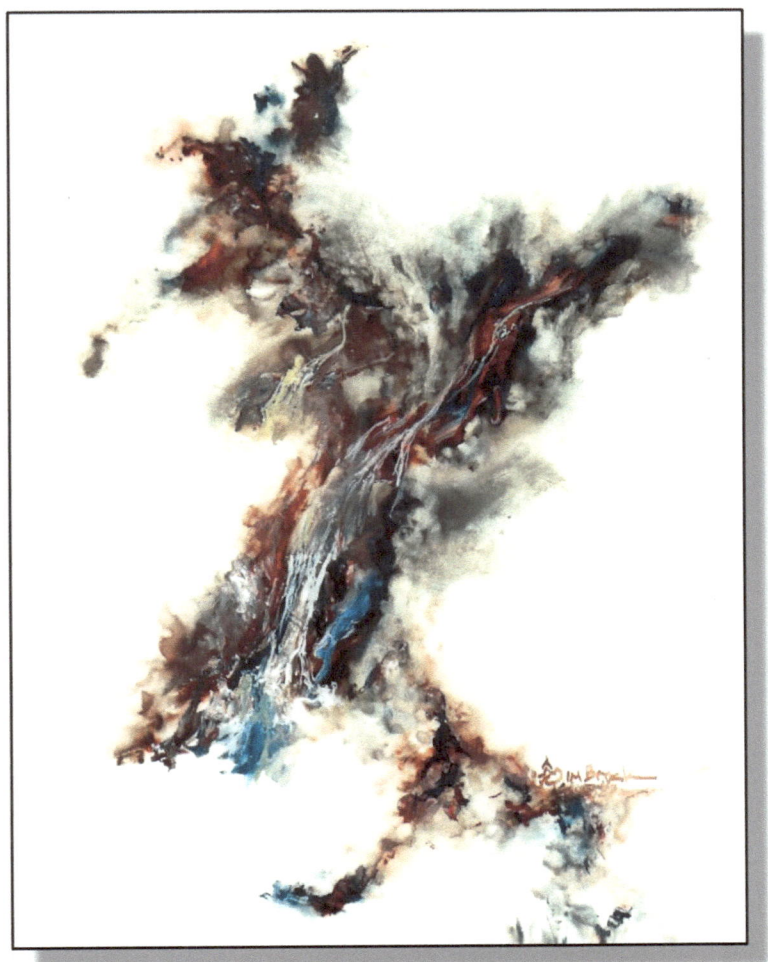

57188 Life Falls

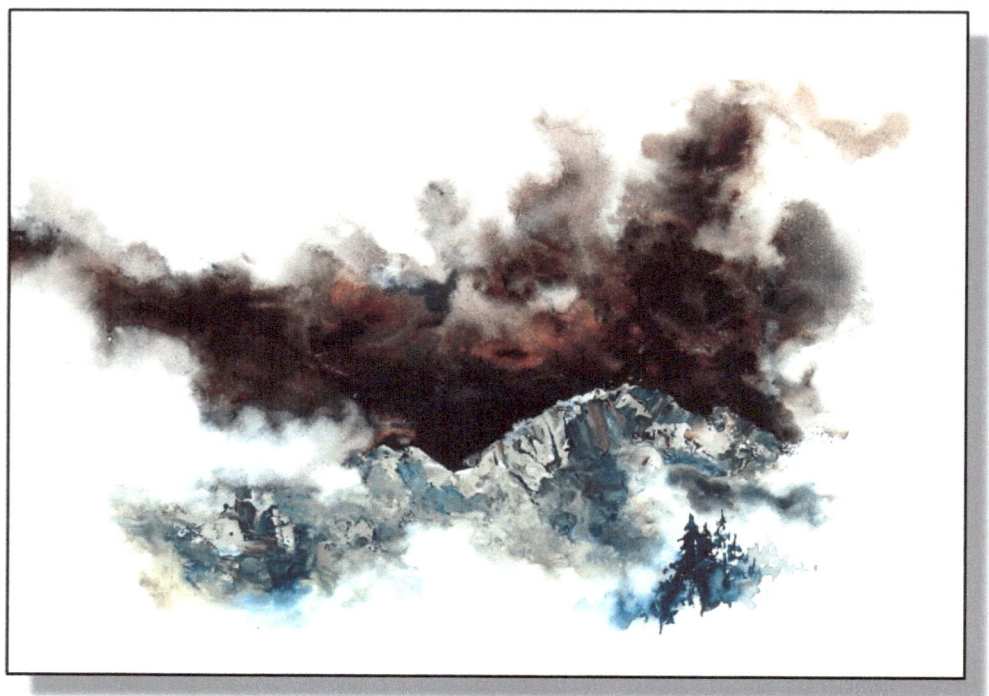

57189 Mountain Storm

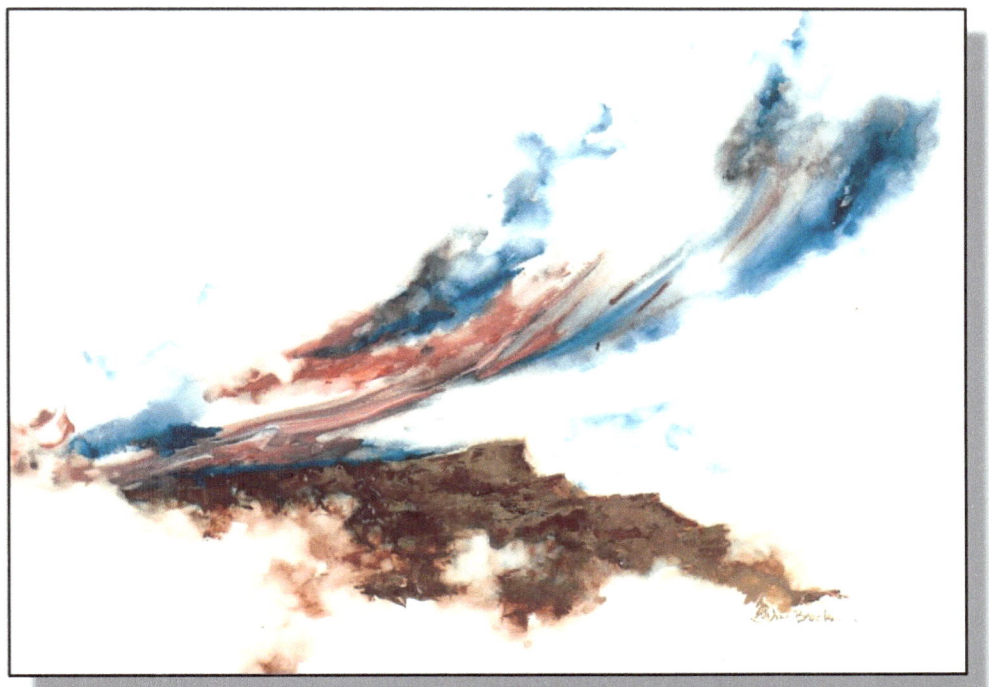

57190 Sunrise

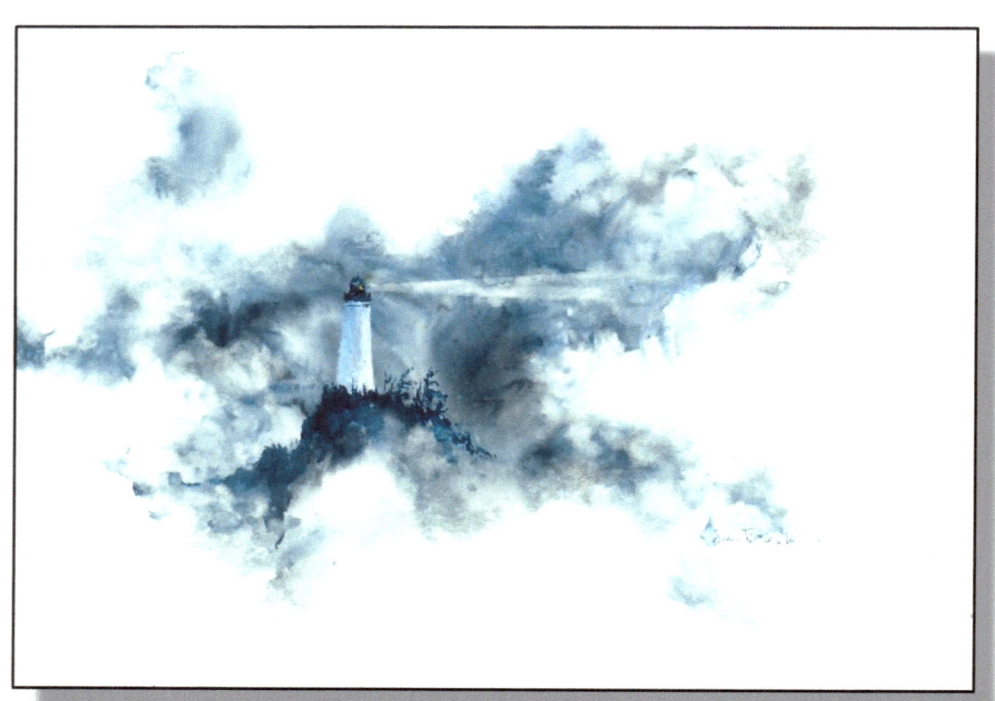

57191 Light Help

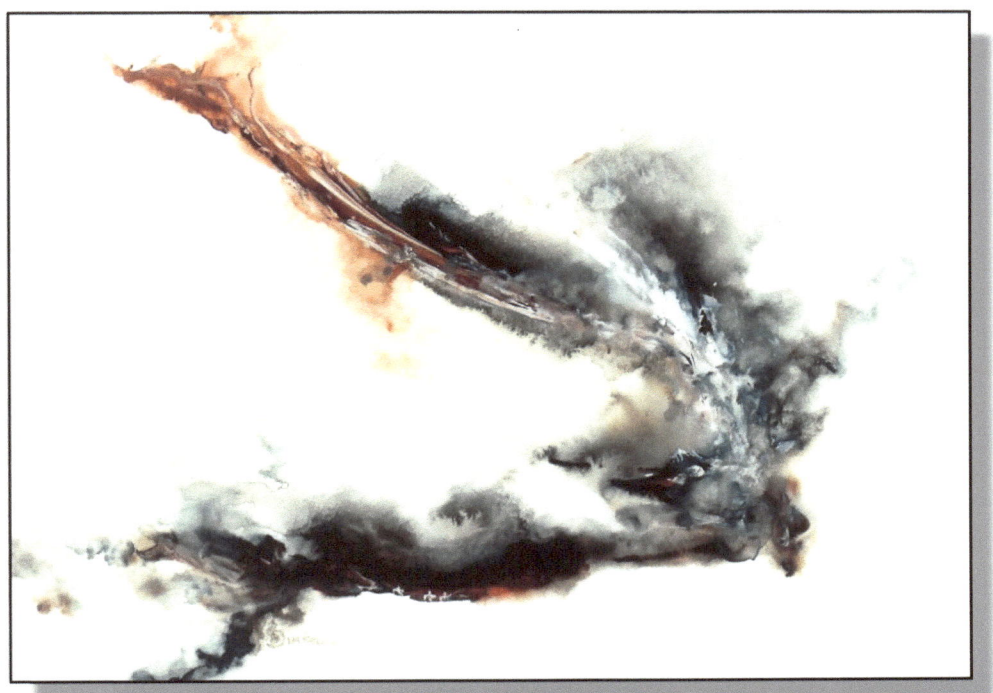

57192 On the Trail

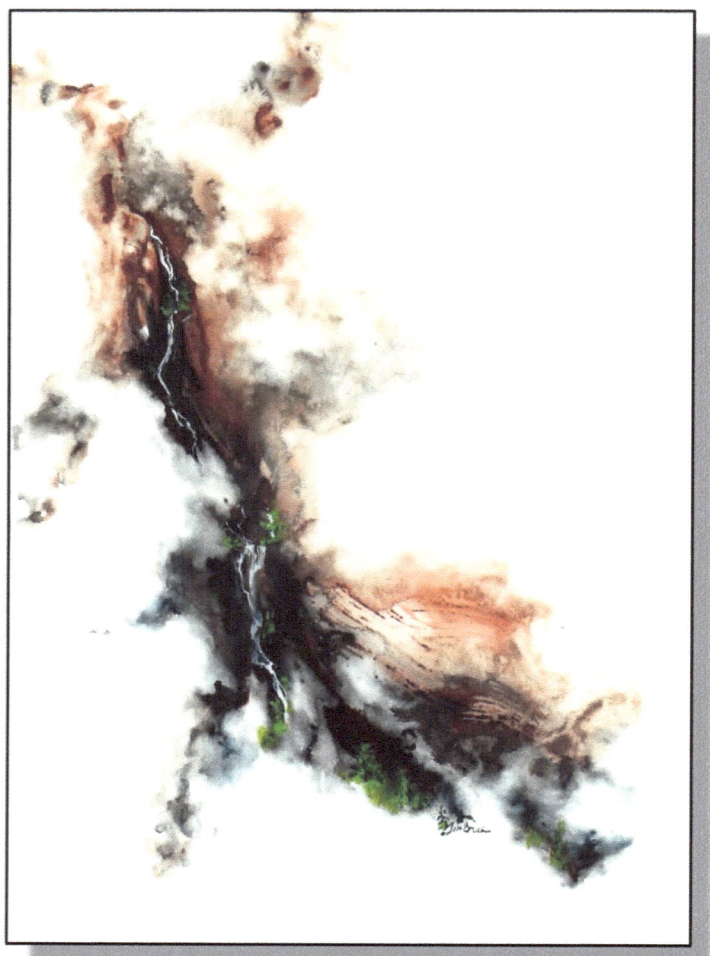

57193 Dark Falls

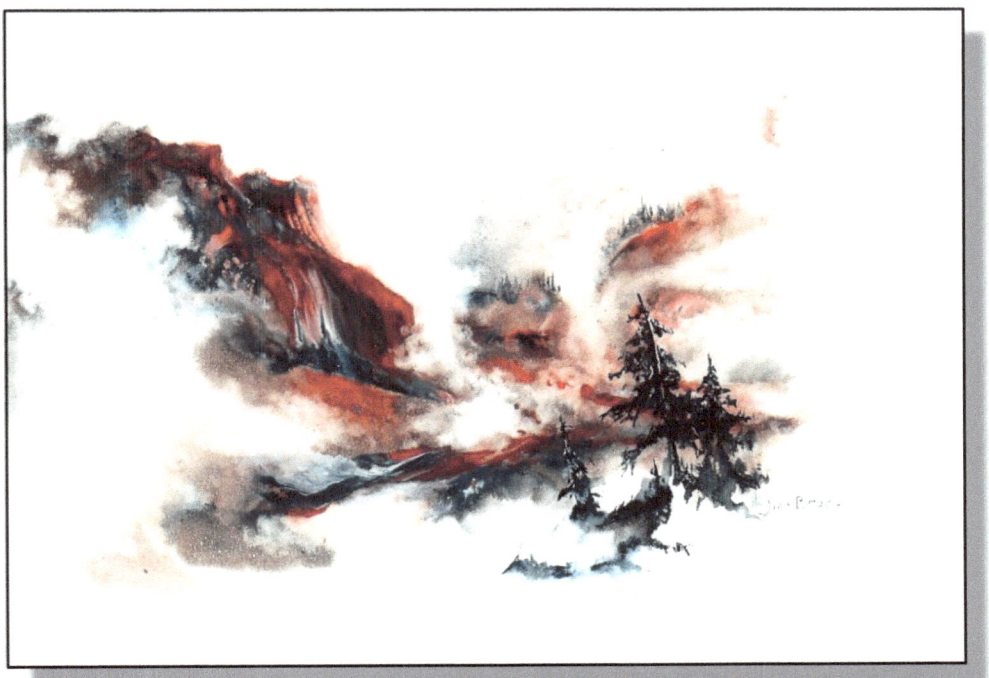

57194 Into Change

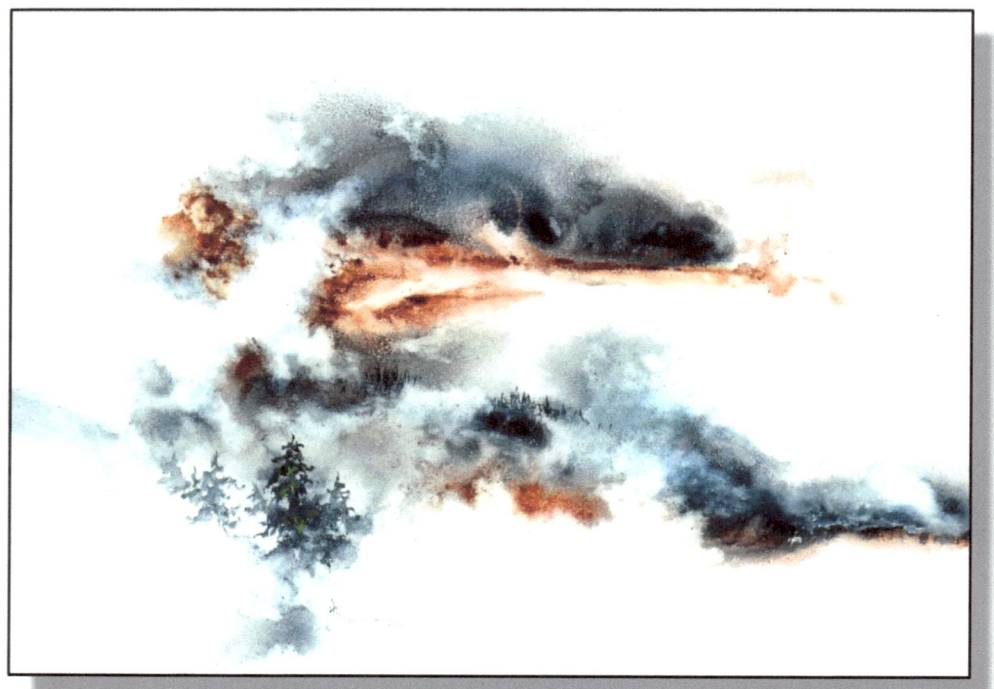

57195 Hope

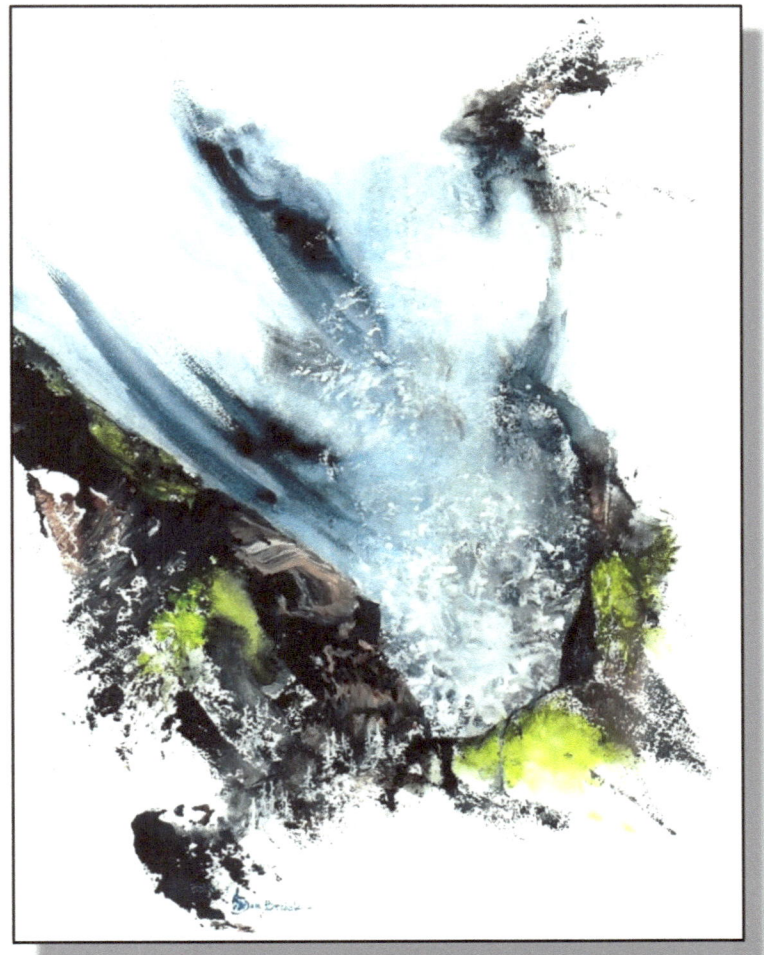

57196 Falls Rim

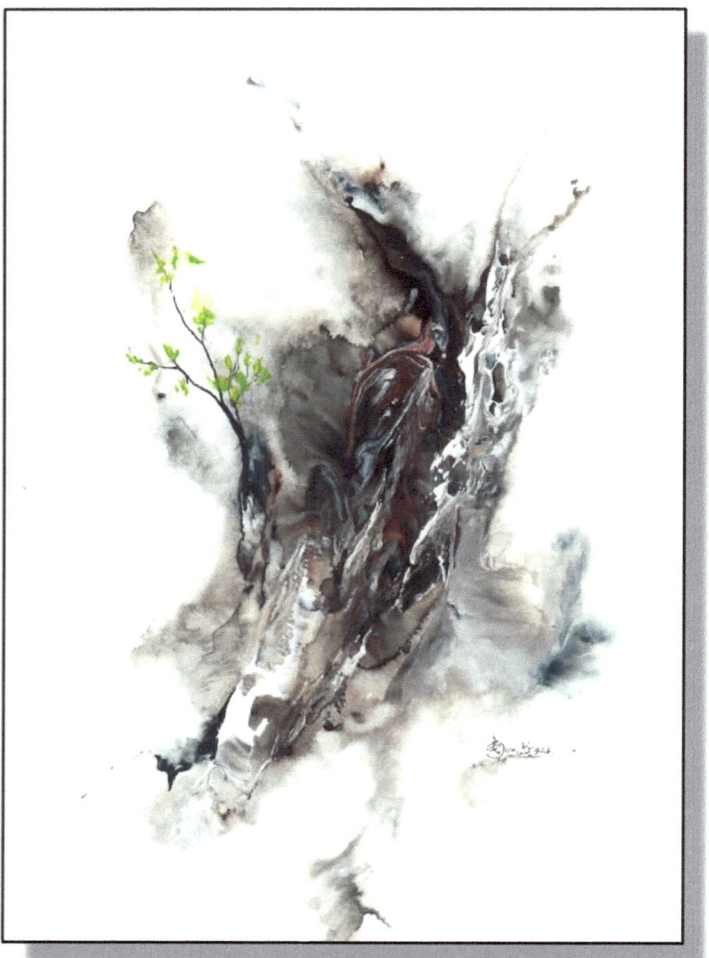

57197 Spring

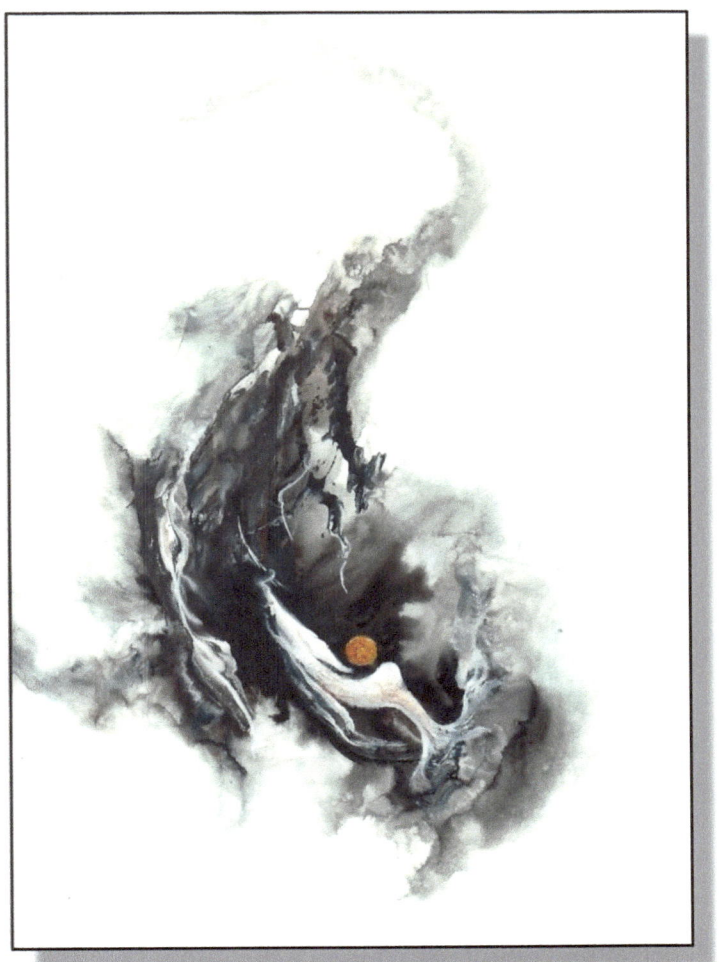

57198 Moon Dance

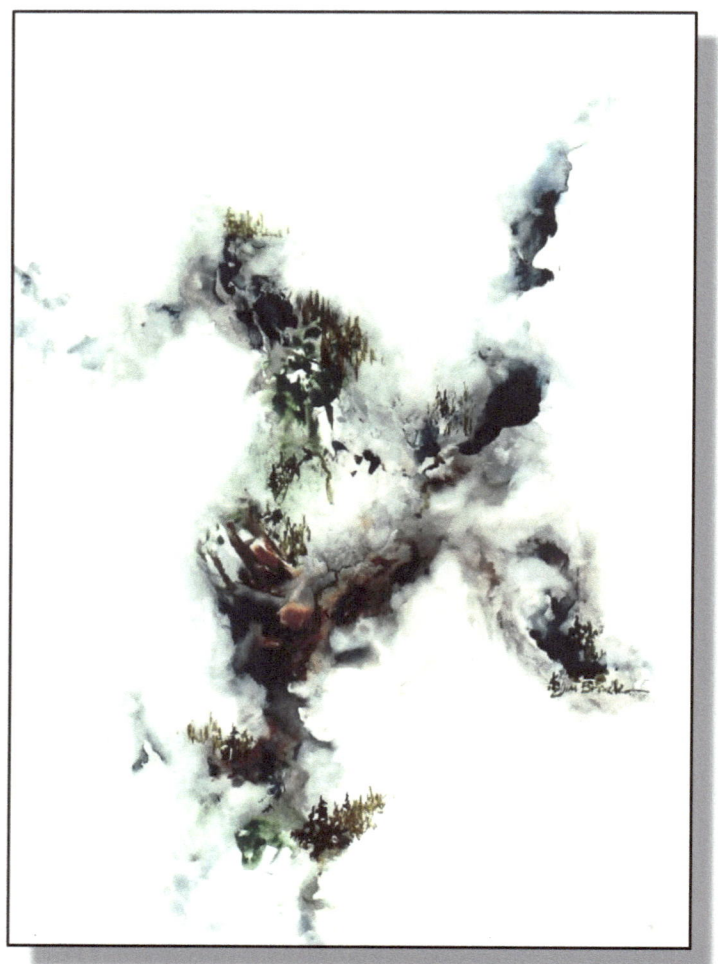

57199 Foggy Pass

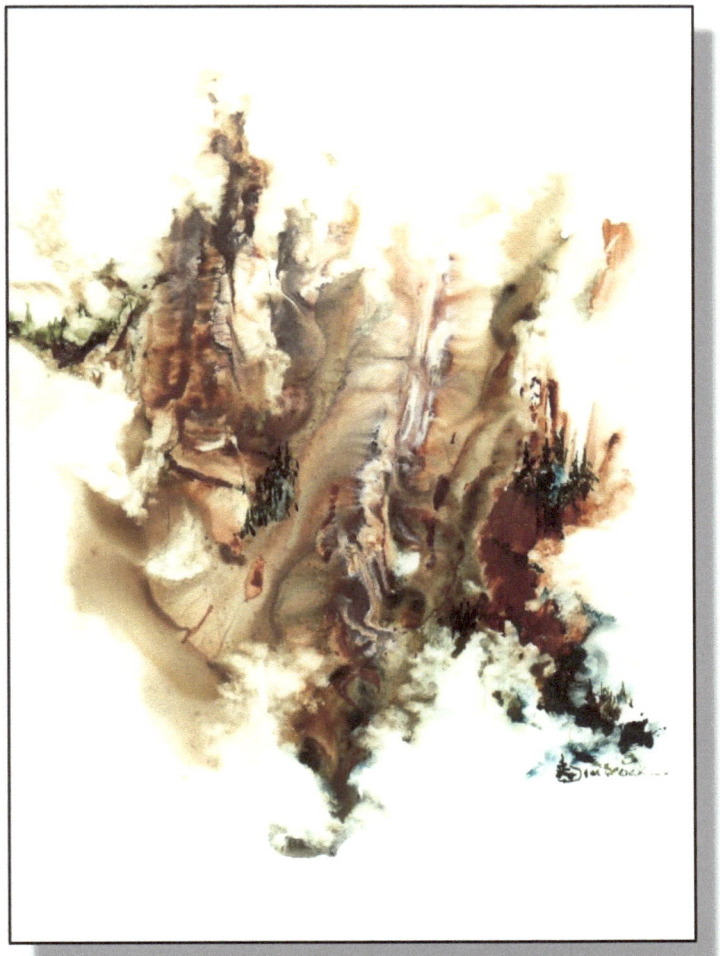

57200 Slum Slide

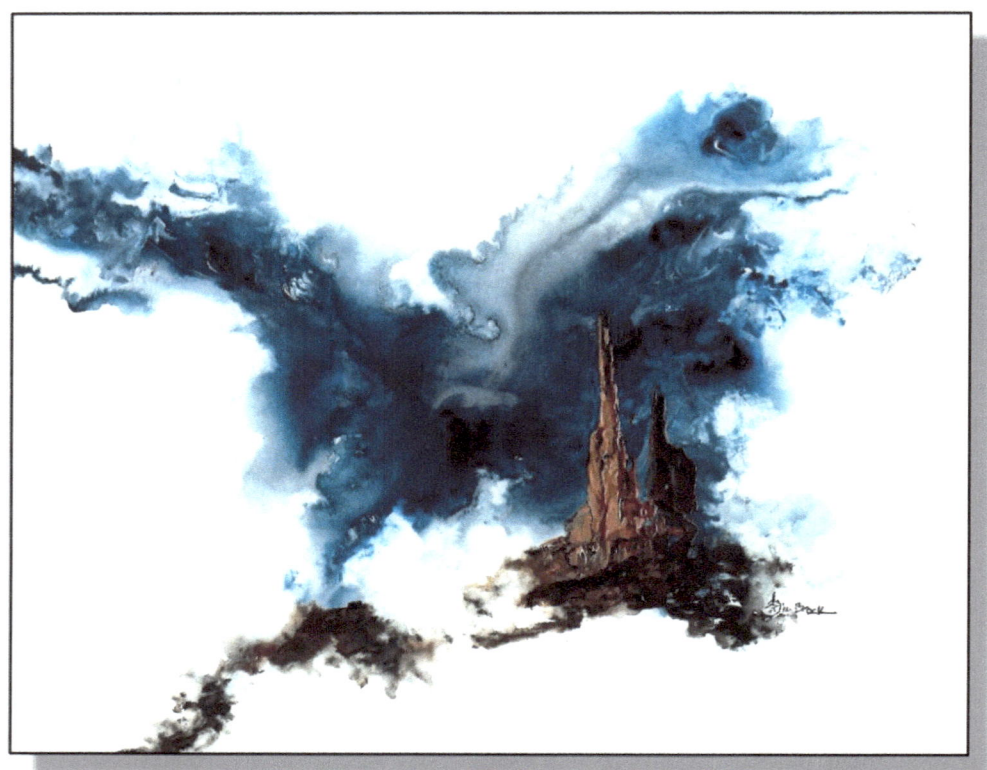

810101 Twilight

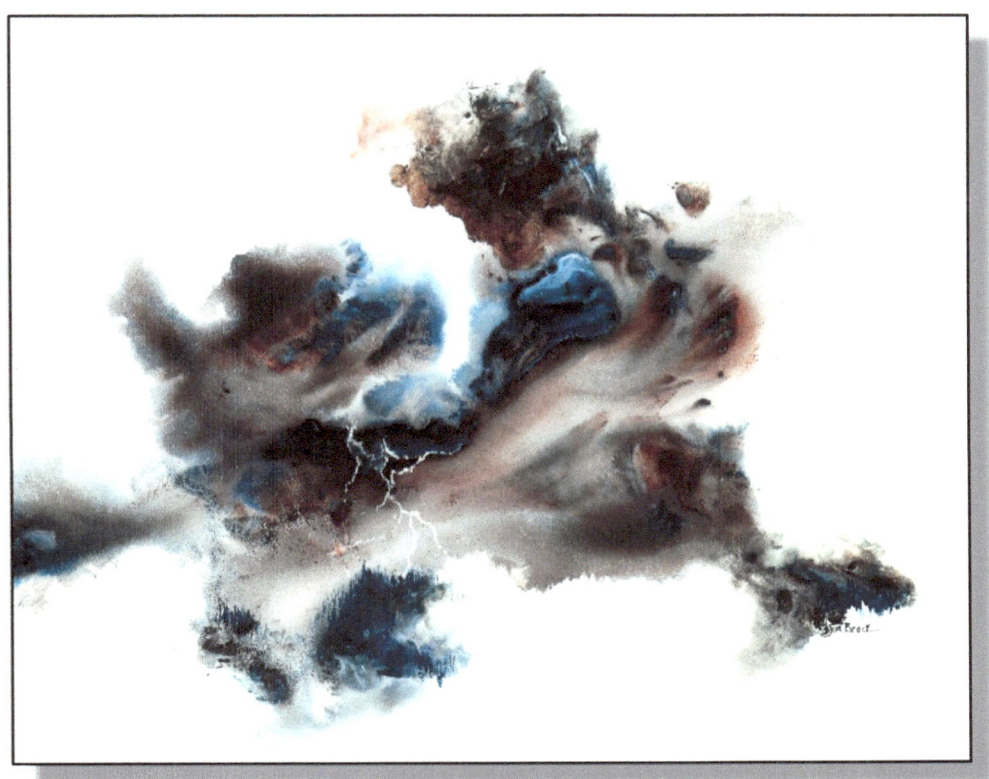

810102 Sunset Storm

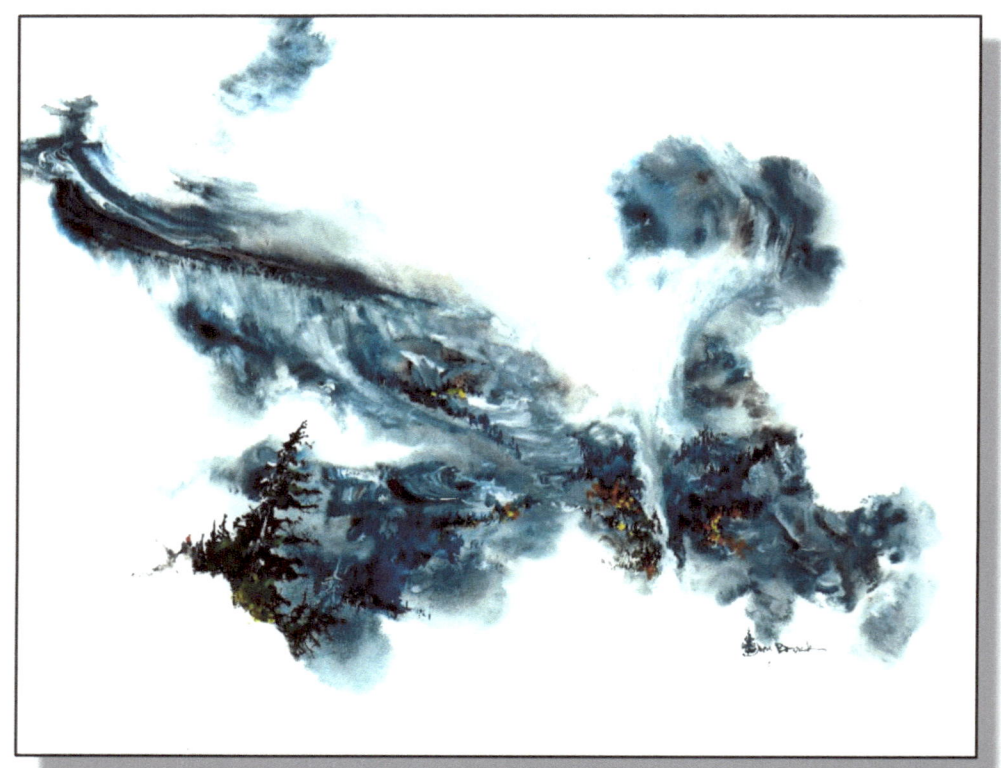

810103 Falls

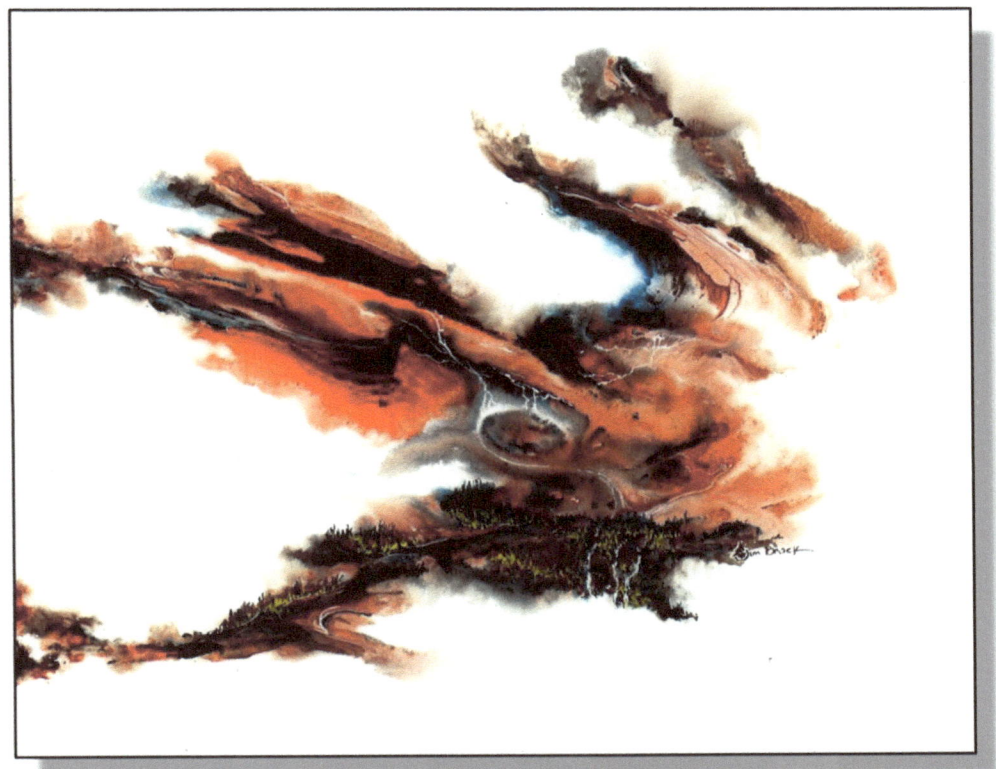

810104 How the Waterfall

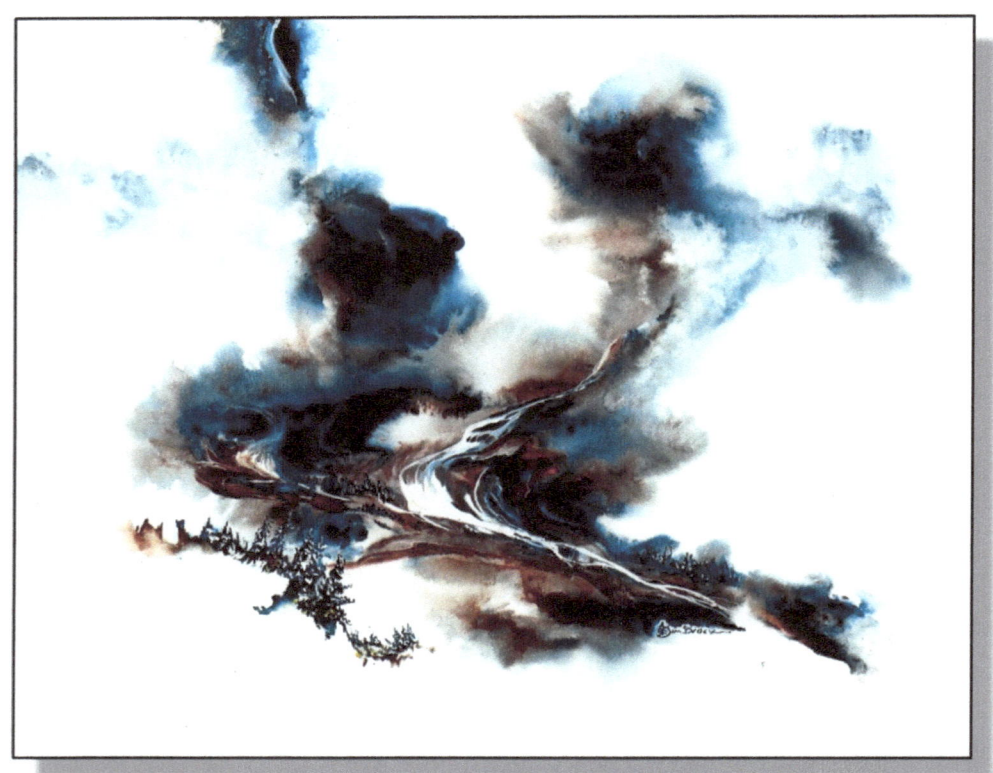

810105 Snow Flow

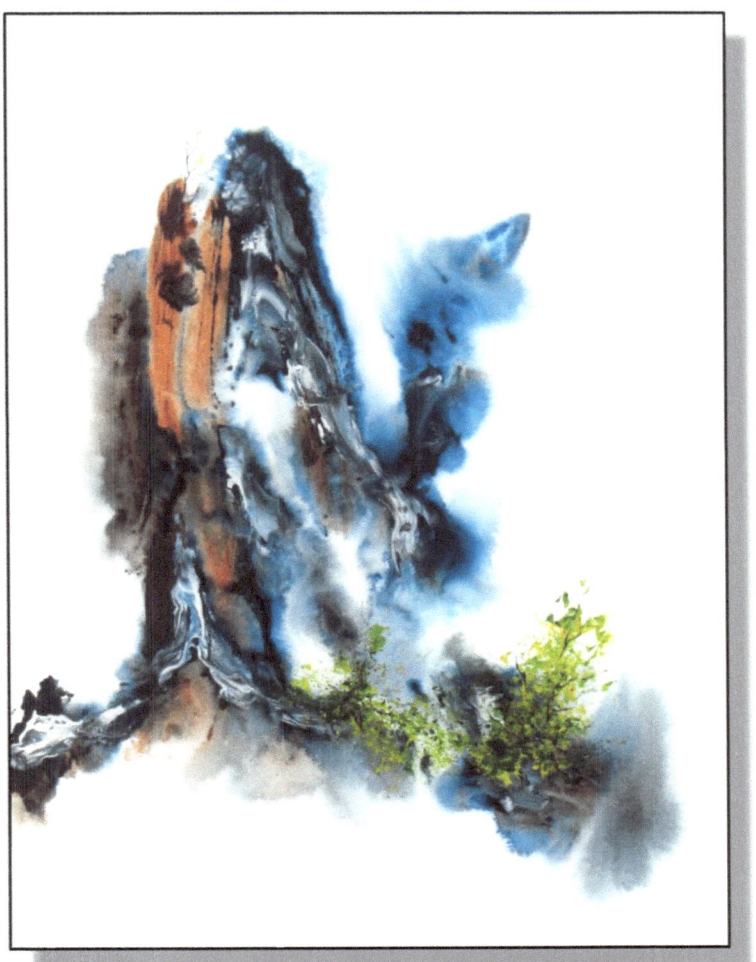

91211 Transformation

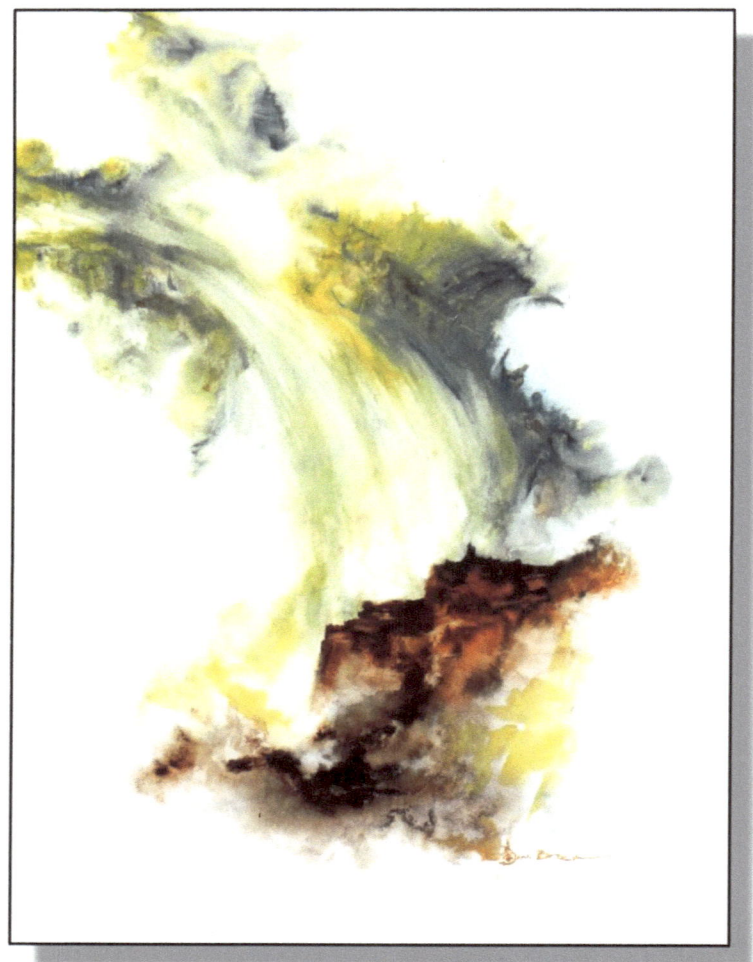

91212 Sky Fall

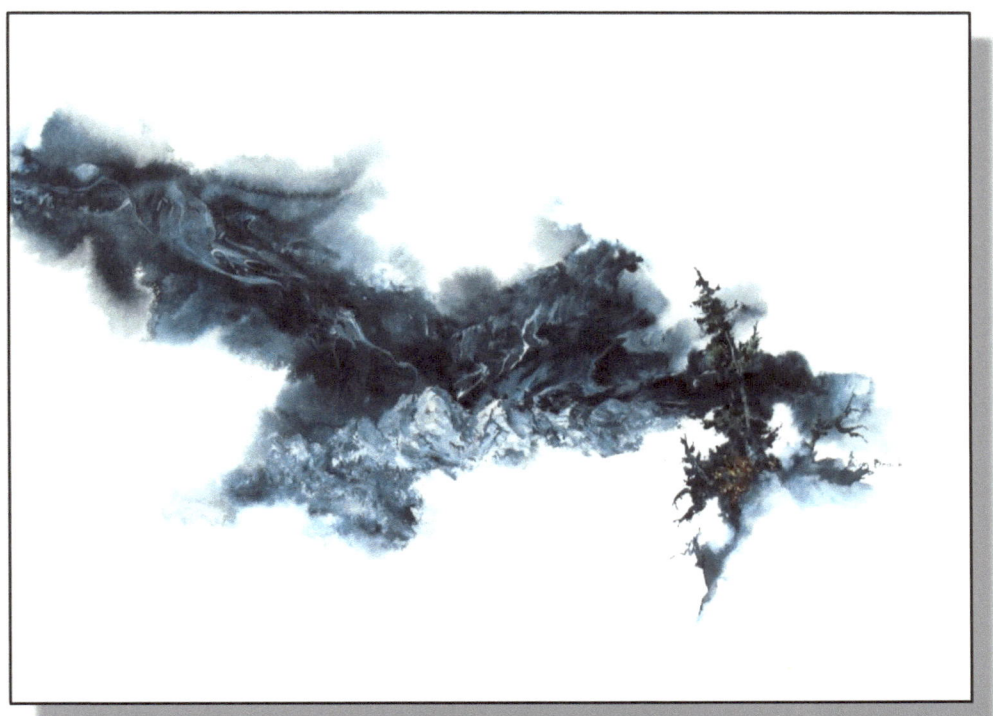

91213 Attractors

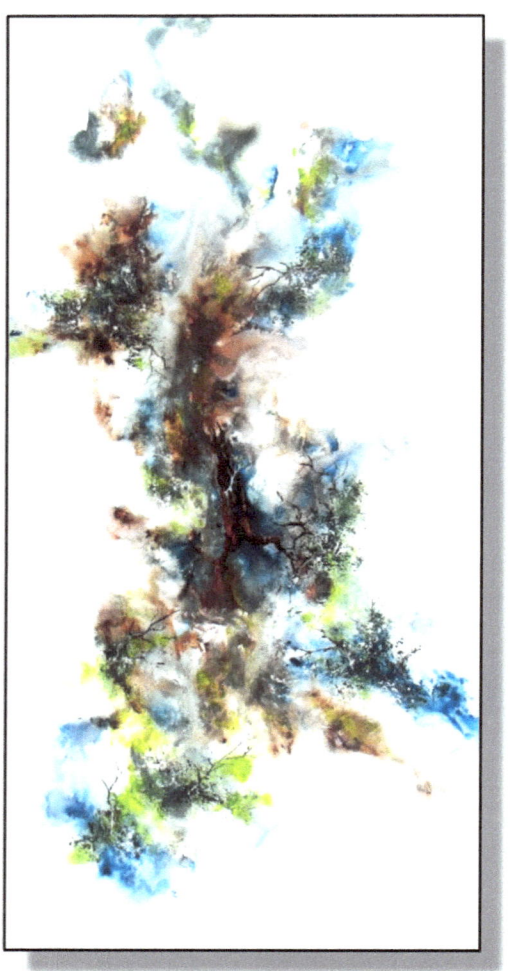

122411Renewal

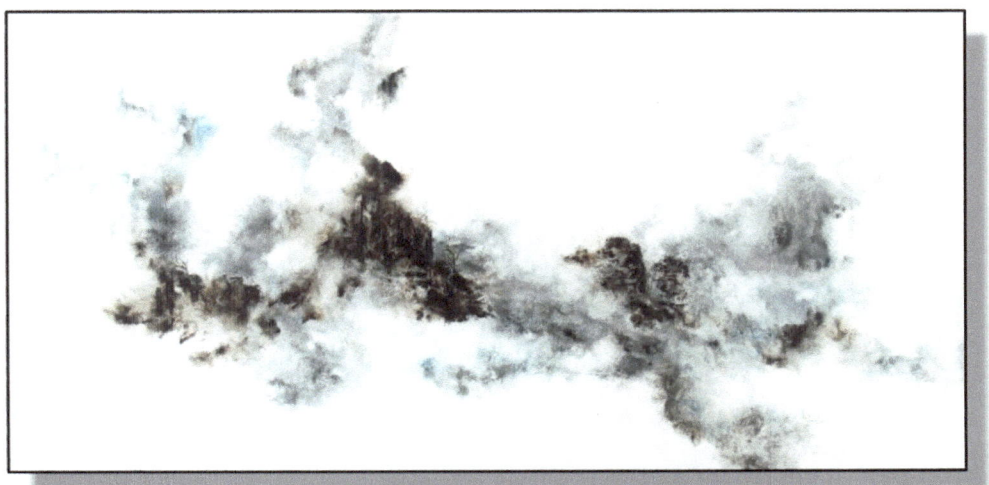

122412 Emergence

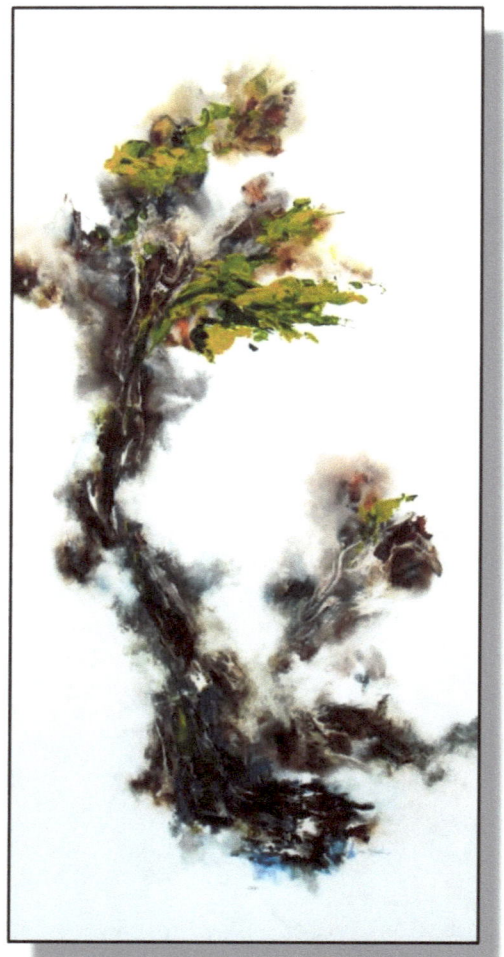

122413 Bloom

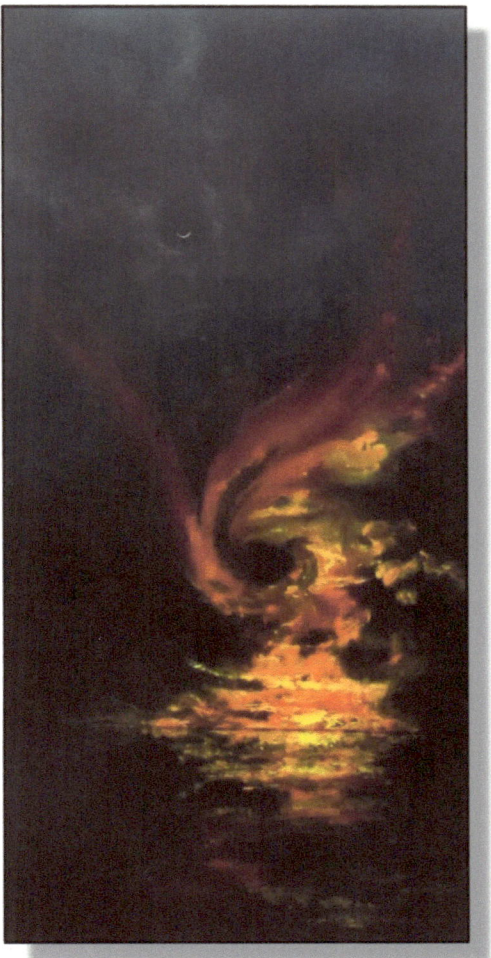

122414 Sunset Moon

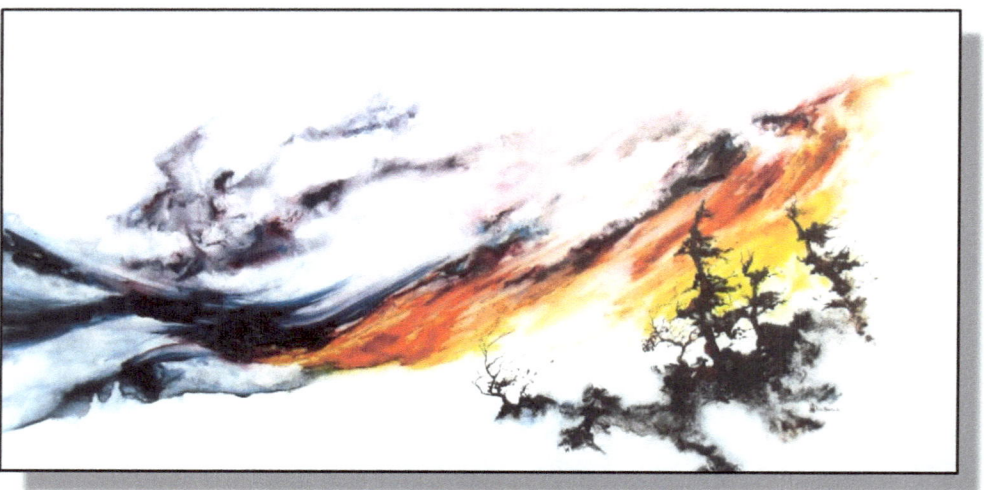

122415 Sunset Wind

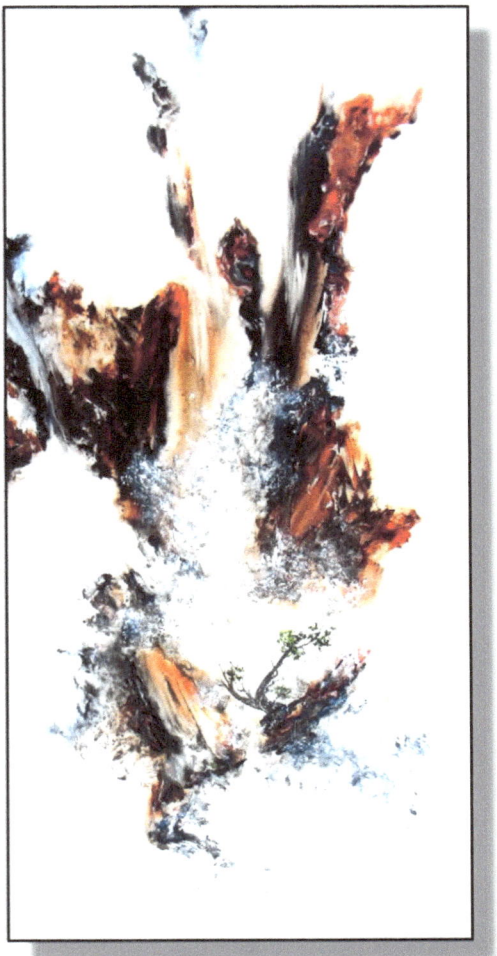

122416 Tumble Falls

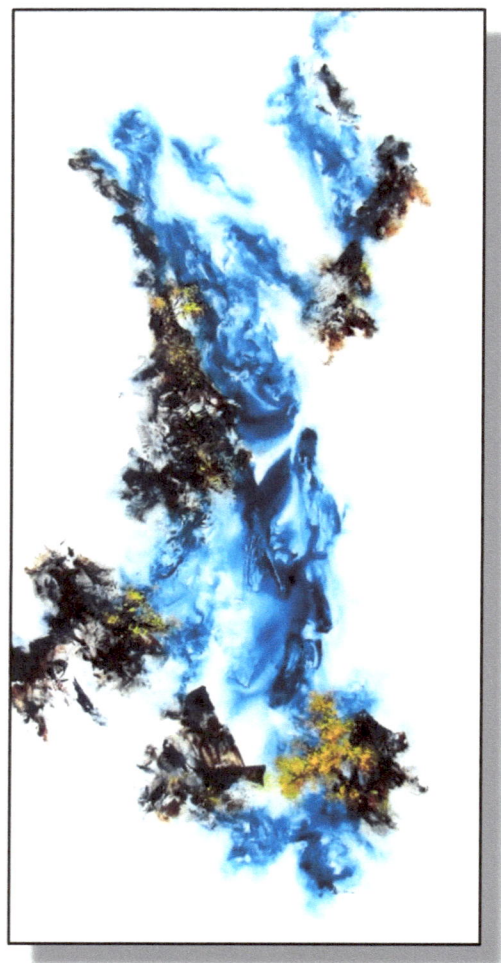

183601 Ice Falls

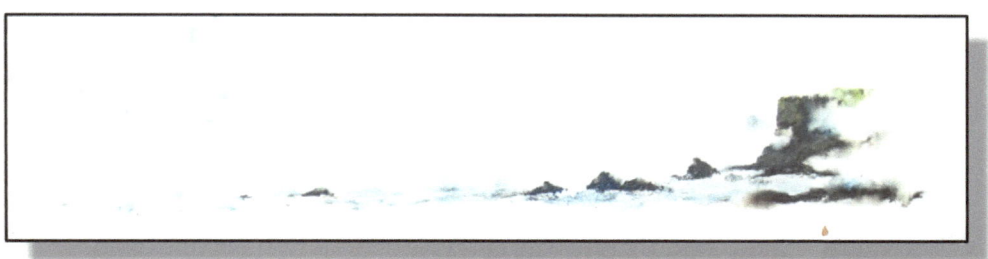

1248101 Pacific

I followed Nowat around the final large painting looking for the way out. After all, Nowat had said that he knew the way.

And there it was, or they were, or…

There were twelve doors there. The last painting's 48 feet had been divided evenly into 12 spaces, each containing a door.

But the doors were not alike—each was a different value of blue. They varied from almost white to a bright, vibrant blue to a very dark, almost black blue. But they were not in any particular order. They were all mixed up. Some dark blue doors were here and there, other light blue there and here.

I turned to Nowat.

"What...what is this?" I mumbled.

Nowat replied, "It's, like, the way out."

"But which one? Which door? I thought you said you knew *A* way out. Are they all a way out?"

"Most assuredly."

"Which do I choose? Is this where there is a prize behind one and a tiger behind the other? I get to be a millionaire or a meal for the tiger? But there are 12 doors."

"I have never, like, seen a tiger."

"Yeah, but I bet there are consequences. Not all doors will make me a millionaire."

"Like, why not?"

"Because that's not the way this works. I know that. Even Goldilocks got into trouble for checking out all the porridge and beds. She had to face the bears because she checked out all her choices."

"Yes, but, like, she got fed and had a nap. What more could she want?"

I turned around to point to the doors. But they had switched order. The lights and darks had all moved around.

"What...what happened? They all moved."

"They do that."

I looked at Nowat and then quickly back at the doors. They had changed order again!

"Aw, come on!" I yelled. "What is this?"

"Like, the way out."

"But, the doors keep changing."

"So?"

"They should stay the same, be consistent, so I could think about them and pick the right one, the safe one."

"But, they are, like, consistent. They are all blue."

"Yeah, but..."

"Like, can't things be consistent and still change?"

"Well...but not like this."

"Like, why not? What do you expect?"

"I expect...well, consistency...?"

"You mean, like, no variation?"

"No, but..."

"So, like, how do you feel about them?"

Then I caught on.

I looked at each door for just a moment, walked up to one of them, grabbed its handle, opened it, and walked through.

***

.

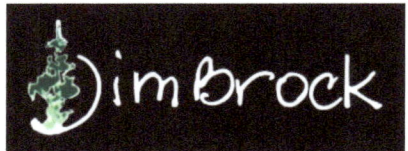

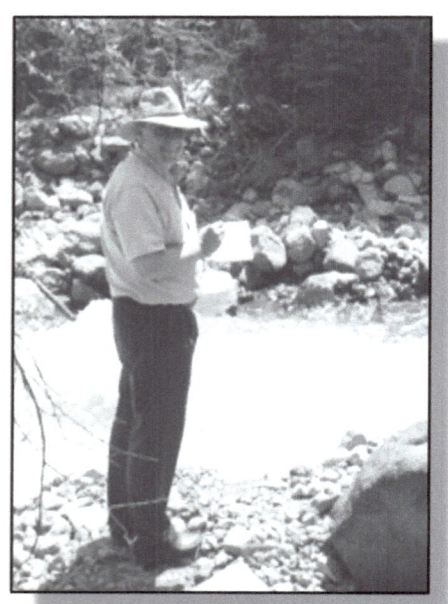

Jim Brock is an award winning professional artist. Over the past 34-plus years, Jim has developed his artistic skills in pencil drawing, Oriental brush painting, and watercolor.

His paintings and drawings are the result of meditations in a world of dualities. He draws inspiration from his surroundings in Western Colorado and Utah as well as from his travels.

Jim is a retired architect, engineer, and Associate Professor Emeritus of Mathematics at Colorado Mesa University.

Further information is available on his web site **www.jim-brock.com**.